AGAINST SCHOOLING

◆

THE RADICAL IMAGINATION SERIES
Edited by Henry A. Giroux and Stanley Aronowitz

Beyond the Spectacle of Terrorism: Global Uncertainty and the Challenge of the New Media,
by Henry A. Giroux (2006)

Global Modernity, by Arif Dirlik (2006)

Left Turn: Forging a New Political Future,
by Stanley Aronowitz (2006)

Stormy Weather: Katrina and the Politics of Disposability,
by Henry A. Giroux (2006)

The Politics of Possibility: Encountering the Radical Imagination,
edited by Gary A. Olson and Lynn Worsham (2007)

The University in Chains: Confronting the Military-Industrial-Academic Complex, by Henry A. Giroux (2007)

Guys and Guns Amok: Domestic Terrorism and School Shootings from the Oklahoma City Bombing to the Virginia Tech Massacre, by Douglas Kellner (2007)

Against Schooling: Toward an Education That Matters,
by Stanley Aronowitz (2008)

Forthcoming

Afromodernity: How Europe Is Evolving Toward Africa,
by Jean Comaroff and John L. Comaroff

AGAINST SCHOOLING
TOWARD AN EDUCATION THAT MATTERS

STANLEY ARONOWITZ

Paradigm Publishers
Boulder • London

Copyright © 2008 Paradigm Publishers

Published in the United States by Paradigm Publishers, 3360 Mitchell Lane, Suite E, Boulder, CO 80301 USA.

Paradigm Publishers is the trade name of Birkenkamp & Company, LLC, Dean Birkenkamp, President and Publisher.

Library of Congress Cataloging-in-Publication Data

Aronowitz, Stanley.
Against schooling: toward an education that matters / Stanley Aronowitz.
    p. cm.—(The radical imagination series; 7)
  Includes bibliographical references and index.
  ISBN 978-1-59451-502-6 (hardcover)
    1. Education—Social aspects—United States. 2. Education—Aims and objectives—United States. 3. Critical pedagogy—United States.
I. Title.

LC191.4.A758   2008
370.11'5—dc22

                      2007052464

Printed and bound in the United States of America on acid-free paper that meets the standards of the American National Standard for Permanence of Paper for Printed Library Materials.

Designed and Typeset by Straight Creek Bookmakers.

12 11 10 09 08   1 2 3 4 5

Contents

◇

Acknowledgments

Chapter 2, "Against Schooling: Education and Social Class": A shorter and somewhat different version first appeared in *Social Text* 22, 2 (Summer 2004).

Chapter 3, "The World Turned Upside Down—Again," is a revised version of a keynote speech I gave to a conference on lifelong learning sponsored by the Ontario Institute of Education, June 21, 2005.

Chapter 4, "Higher Education as a Public Good": A somewhat different version first appeared in *Not for Sale: In Defense of Public Goods*, edited by Anatole Anton, Milton Fisk, and Nancy Holstrom (Boulder, CO: Westview Press, 2000).

Chapter 5, "Subaltern in Paradise": A somewhat different version was published in *The Subaltern Speak: Curriculum, Power, and Educational Struggles*, edited by Michael W. Apple and Kristen L. Buras (New York: Routledge, 2006).

Chapter 6, "Academic Unionism and the Future of Higher Education," first appeared in *Will Teach for Food: Academic Labor in Crisis*, edited by Cary Nelson (Minneapolis: University of Minnesota Press, 1997). Reprinted with permission.

Chapter 7, "Should Academic Unions Get Involved in Governance?" is a somewhat different version of an article that appeared in *Liberal Education* (Spring 2007).

Chapter 9, "Gramsci and Education," was first published in somewhat different form in *Gramsci and Education*, edited by Carmel Borg, Joseph Buttigieg, and Peter Mayo (Lanham, MD: Rowman and Littlefield, 2003).

Chapter 10, "Paulo Freire's Radical Democratic Humanism," first appeared in *Paulo Freire: A Critical Encounter*, edited by Peter McLaren and Peter Leonard (New York: Routledge, 1992).

◊

Introduction

In the era when mass schooling has reached all levels of the
education hierarchy—most recently "higher education"—institutions and their staffs are under tremendous pressure to deliver
credentials that assist students to obtain better jobs than would
be available to them without the diploma, certificate, or degree.
The drive to link schooling to the occupational structure is not
new but has recently acquired more urgency than ever before as
working- and middle-class people experience the world as more
dangerous and more uncertain. Obtaining a berth for their child
in kindergarten no less than college is now a major issue for
many. Panic overwhelms us, and not primarily because of the
so-called terrorism threat. Many of us fear obliteration in bald
economic terms even more than in relation to the determination
of political authorities to plunge the United States into permanent
war. In fact, as always, a significant portion of the young perceive
war as an opportunity. An opportunity for what? For obtaining
free schooling and that precious credential—and perhaps, in an
insecure world, a measure of economic security.

Make no mistake. From the perspective of the effectiveness of
its domestic rule, contrary to the conventional wisdom, the power
of U.S. capitalism does not reside chiefly in its ability to provide
good jobs, decent living standards for most, and a sense that the
future is secure and promises happiness for the overwhelming
majority of the population. Living standards have certainly risen
since World War II, but at the turn of the twenty-first century,
our collective sense of well-being has never been more precarious.
Historically, many Americans have enjoyed an unprecedented
measure of "material comfort" if by that term we mean that most
have enough to eat, a roof over their heads, a private means of
transportation that in most parts of the country is a necessity
rather than a luxury, and some kind of employment or a pension

of sorts. But today many are deeply worried about their circumstances, and this uneasiness is due to a widespread anxiety about the future not only of their children but of themselves. Despite working harder and longer, often sacrificing huge chunks of their free time by working two or three jobs in order to maintain the historical level of material culture, many are simply unable to make ends meet without plunging into crippling debt.

In fact, the credit system is supporting the economy and is sustained by the fiction that loans extended for consumption are almost sure to be paid back. If they are not, banks and other corporate lenders have raised interest rates to more than 30 percent for the least-qualified borrowers in order to ensure that the lenders will not lose on forfeitures or bankruptcies. For example, the easy credit that sustained the housing bubble for the past decade and a half has already burst; the inability of at least one-sixth (some experts calculate one-quarter) of recent borrowers to meet their mortgage payments has resulted in a huge foreclosure rate even though many of these deals required borrowers to pay only the interest on the mortgage. As I write, many banks have already introduced draconian standards for granting credit, not only to the least financially qualified borrowers but also to fairly reliable loan risks. Sales of new homes have dropped for the first time in more than fifteen years, and sales of previously owned homes are also in the dumps. Congress is preparing to impose tighter restrictions on what many in the industry believe was a highly irresponsible regime of mortgage lending. That home prices zoomed in the midst of the easy credit that prompted dizzying home sales in the first five years of the new century deterred neither borrowers nor lending institutions because many new "homeowners" were paying subprime rates or paying only the interest on their loans. When, according to agreements, the payment schedule reverted from "interest only" to the principal and monthly payments skyrocketed, hundreds of thousands of borrowers defaulted on their loans and lost their homes—and there is no end in sight. Sales of new homes declined substantially in fall 2006 and in January 2007 registered a 16.9 percent drop over the previous month. Since fall 2006, prices have been reduced by as much as 25 percent in some regions. Similarly, from the late 1990s to 2005, auto corporations offered zero percent or below-prime-rate finance charges to buyers wishing to purchase high-end vehicles such as SUVs and full-sized cars. These sales plummeted with the spike in gas prices, and the big-three automakers experienced drastically lower profits in 2006 as sales declined. In May 2007, one of the industry's icons, Chrysler, was sold to a financial corporation by Daimler, which, after five years of declining profits, finally concluded that the risks were too great. Despite assurances to workers that the company would not be dismantled and sold in pieces and that further layoffs are not in the offing, the new owners will have to cut costs, and labor is the most likely candidate for the chopping block. By summer 2007, the United Auto Workers, the union of the industry's largest parts supplier, Delphi, had made major wage and benefits concessions, setting an unprecedented new pattern of a two-tier wage system that the major car companies have seized upon. These were followed in September and October by similar concessions at General Motors (GM) and Chrysler. The GM agreement transferred $50 billion of liabilities for health benefits to the union but promised payments of only $35 billion, in stages. In addition, the deal established a two-tier wage system, once viewed by the union as anathema. In return, the corporation promised to retain the 73,000-person labor force, but a parallel Chrysler agreement failed to offer such guarantees and, as a result, generated considerable opposition among the 45,000 members of the union.

The so-called middle class (at least in terms of consumption) harbors a haunting fear of falling into poverty as the old notion that perhaps a majority of the population has a stable income rapidly vanishes. Many who might have been counted in that category are experiencing uncertainty about their jobs and discovering that their incomes simply can no longer sustain their once secure living standard. Although the official poverty index identifies about 40 million at or below the phantom line of about $20,000 a year for a household of four, tens of millions hover at or below the minimum "comfort" line that, according to some studies of people apart from the major cities on two coasts, is at least double that figure. In New York City's four boroughs outside Manhattan, the minimum comfort line is around $55,000 for a household of four. In New York City, where a good union wage is about $20 an hour and many workers earn much less, the two- or three-paycheck family is necessary to pay the bills for ever-rising housing, food, transportation, health, and education costs. In many instances, only "easy" high-interest credit keeps body and soul together unless, for example, a humongous medical bill wipes out the fragile balances needed to reproduce everyday existence at a level above desperation. Yet, as C. Wright Mills remarked more than fifty years ago, most of us experience our feelings of discontent and uncertainty as "private troubles" rather than as issues to be addressed publicly and col-lectively. The power of the system is its capacity to effectively pro-mulgate the myth that our fate is, in the last instance, individual; that collective action to address our troubles is futile or at best can result in only temporary amelioration. And we are victims of an overweening sense of fatality (in the words of Doris Day's popular rendition of the song "Que Sera, Sera," "the future's not ours to see ... what will be, will be").

Although there is still plenty of work in some regions of the country, money is tight, and good jobs are scarce, if by "good job" we mean labor that offers security, a decent income, benefits, and interesting tasks. But part of the prevailing hype is that getting a credential in some technical field such as health care, computers, or one of the building or mechanical trades is likely to overcome the vicissitudes of the job market. With some justification, in an era of deindustrialization during which whole regions of the Northeast and Midwest and, more recently, the textiles-saturated Southeast have been laid waste, students from working-class, managerial, and professional backgrounds believe that beyond high school, further academic and technical schooling is mandatory for any expectation of beating the massive restructuring that is occurring in the nature of work. The half-life of an acquired set of compe-tencies is now less than five years, and the permanent job has been relegated to a distant memory. The rapidly changing struc-tural organization and the steady erosion of income connected to manufacturing, clerical, and retail employment make "jobs" less secure and remunerative. As a collectivity, we have come to conflate education and schooling and have placed our hopes for a secure, if not a bright, future in the credentialing process. Few of even the so-called educators ask the question: What matters beyond the reading, writing, and numeracy that are presumably taught in the elementary and secondary grades? The old question of what a kid needs to become an informed "citizen" capable of participating in making the large and small public decisions that affect the larger world as well as everyday life receives honorable mention but not serious consideration. These unasked questions are symptoms of a new regime of educational expectations that privileges job readiness above any other educational values.

But in recent years, illiteracy, once believed to have been solved by universal public schooling, has once more become a public issue. First of all, the population has grown faster than the resources available for public goods, especially education.

The Bush administration's No Child Left Behind program, a largely unfunded mandate for state and local authorities to meet a series of standards determined by test scores of elementary school children, has raised the stakes of language learning. The quasi-official policy of the federal Department of Education is that phonics is a superior technique to whole-language learning; consequently, the department rewards local school districts that adopt the technique, regardless of whether or not research has shown its comparative effectiveness. At the same time, teachers are obliged to administer reading, writing, and numeracy tests to children in grades two through eight. Under these circumstances, "teaching to test" dominates the curriculum and pedagogy. To the extent that the teacher is transformed from an intellectual into a technician, the long-term intention of educational conservatives is to make the classroom teacher-proof. Thus, parallel to the tendency of work rationalization in other sectors to deskill many occupations, teaching is rapidly losing its professional content. Whether intentional or not, having denied the value of creative pedagogy and teacher classroom autonomy, the effect of No Child Left Behind and its local variants has been to introduce the teacherless curriculum, in which there is little or no room for interpretation and creativity.

As the student becomes an adult, she is expected to lead a more or less privatized existence, raising children, worrying about personal health and bills, with her participation confined to commodity consumption. Reading as a form of pleasure and writing as a form of self-expression or analytic communication are increasingly reserved for an ever-diminishing coterie of "accidental" intellectuals—accidental because there is little either in the curriculum or in the pedagogy of public education that encourages what was once termed the "general" reader, a person who, whatever her occupation or profession, remains curious about the larger world, cares about politics, and tries to stay current with events and new ideas. Now we have lowered our expectations of our children—and their expectations as well—and, in our anxiety for their economic fate, lowered our own: We no longer strive to help them fulfill the ancient liberal hope that the next generation will help shape a better world, let alone the radical dream of creating a world without exploitation and oppression—a world without poverty, ignorance, and disease. Ours is a time in which, except for the sole decision of who should rule us—the act of voting that is perennially equated with democracy—minimalism has seized the day. Always prone to wealth envy, we have elevated the rich and famous to the status of folk heroes. Even as young people aspire to no more than the next rung on the occupational ladder or to equal their parents' social and economic standing, in contradictory fashion they carry the not-so-secret lust for wealth and fame, a lust that will eventually make them avid lottery players and gamblers in other, less benign forms. Even as the fabled disparity between rich and poor increasingly marks our society, the class divide in schooling grows wider. In the quest to secure their children's future, "middle-class" parents barely hesitate to acquire hefty debt to pay private school and college tuition, whereas few of the working class can obtain such loans. Those who have endured the trials of postsecondary schooling often know that seeking their child's admission into a "selective" institution is less about acquiring real knowledge than gaining cultural and social capital. They want their kids to be able to identify cultural signs that mark an educated individual—knowing the right authors, the titles of their books, and the latest cultural vocabulary; having vague familiarity with "top-forty" classical music; and gaining some knowledge of the leading ideas of film theory that are rapidly displacing the older literary references. If the school is in the top three hundred, students are intent on making social contacts that might at some future date lead to jobs, especially in finance and management. For the rest of the 4,200 institutions of higher education, achieving a credential signifies mainly that the student is more or less reliably integrated into the work-world system. She shows up on time, hands in assignments according to the instructions, and sits for exams. In a large number of instances, as in most public high schools, educational achievement is measured by student performance on multiple-choice tests, a practice dictated by bulging registration in many disciplines, especially at entry level, and the shortage of full-time faculty. Until their junior and senior years, students, even in some research universities, do not write research papers; indeed, in the four-year public colleges, many students never write a long paper and barely learn how to use a library. When taken together with the fact that these conditions also prevail at the high school level, it is not uncommon for a student to graduate with a bachelor's or even master's degree without having ever written more than a short paper. He will almost never be required to produce a large research paper—a senior thesis, for example—as a condition of graduation from college.

Most state colleges and universities—which about 70 percent of all higher-education students attend—have adopted the organizational trappings of medium-sized or large corporations: Many services are outsourced to private contractors, including instruction. From food service to building maintenance to instruction, the permanent institutional staff has been cut to the bone—except management, which has grown enormously in the past two decades. In some institutions, the deans, vice presidents, and directors of programs are the fastest-growing occupations, and their salary levels often exceed those of the highest-paid professors by as much as 100 percent.

Today it is the rare non-doctoral-degree-granting institution that does not contract with adjunct labor to teach many, if not most, of its courses. The part-timer is typically not a regular member of the tenure-bearing faculty. She is hired on a semester, or at best a yearly, basis and, except where collective bargaining has provided some continuity of employment, may be discharged at the will of a department chair or other academic officer. That the adjunct teacher may possess a PhD or another postgraduate credential does not obviate the fact that he is a contractor rather than an employee and, from the perspective of academic institutional citizenship, is all but excluded from the community.

Once the adjunct professor was a specialist in a particular profession who offered courses that would otherwise not be given by the traditional undergraduate and graduate disciplinary faculty. These include offerings in law; accounting; architecture; and a number of specific sciences such as ecology, geology, and meteorology. Now, at a time when only 29 percent of recent faculty positions are tenure-track, the adjunct has become the bedrock of the curriculum. In some public and private universities and colleges alike, 40 to 60 percent of the courses are taught by part-timers. In turn, since adjunct rates are not prorated to full-time salaries, in order to make a living the part-timer teaches more than a full teaching load, frequently racing from department to department or campus to campus. As I argue in Chapter 5, the adjunct professor is the subaltern of higher education.

The proliferation of the part-timers raises several questions: Why have colleges and universities turned to adjunctification? How can the institutions get away with fulfilling their curricular needs with part-timers, even as tuition prices exceed the inflation rate? What is the source of the tens of thousands of qualified professors who are forced to earn their living as part-timers, a condition that usually brings contempt from the administration and even from the full-time faculty, overwork, and poor psychic as well as economic remuneration? And what are the implications of this regime for education as opposed to training and credentialing?

Before considering these questions, I want to sound a cautionary note. In no way would I deny the quality of adjunct teachers or their dedication to the educational enterprise. In the overwhelming majority of instances, finding oneself in the subaltern position of part-time instructor has nothing to do with ability or even achievement. Many part-timers are superb teachers, accomplished authors, and skilled mentors. If about 70 percent of those who seek employment as professors are destined for part-time status, their fate is not chiefly their own doing except for the decision to remain in college teaching regardless of the circumstances that reduce them to poorly paid contractors, a choice that can be explained in various ways. One explanation is the partial fiction that higher education remains the guardian of enlightenment, the one area in which the intellect, however much it is regularly degraded by the material conditions of teaching and learning, still corresponds to the stated mission of the institution. Another is that a growing army of part-timers holds doctorates, hard-won degrees with all the talents that are implied by this station, an achievement they are loathe to abandon. Then there is the problem mentioned previously: There are few good jobs in the private sector, and those that still exist are disappearing even as I write.

Which raises the question of why the humanities, arts, and social sciences in particular, but also the so-called hard sciences, have overproduced PhDs, and master's in fine arts, still the reigning credential for art and music teachers. After all, academics no less than plumbers are aware that their salaries and conditions depend, in great measure, on limiting the supply of labor, and since the PhD is the union card for a tenured position in higher education, the first line of defense should be to reduce the number of admissions to these programs. The second line would be to raise the bar for completion by a series of exams of which the dissertation is the pinnacle. Obviously most if not all graduate programs have disdained such rigor in favor of a rather unacknowledged drive for productivity. As Mark Bosquet has brilliantly argued, the chief reason for this decision is cheap labor. Graduate teaching assistants and adjuncts teach the bulk of courses in colleges and universities for wages that are barely a fraction of those of the full-time faculty. In elite as well as second- and third-tier institutions, they are indispensable. The fiction that graduate students are serving some kind of apprenticeship under the mentorship of experienced full-time faculty may have satisfied the likes of the National Labor Relations Board, but those on the ground are not fooled. The full-time faculty teaches the grad students and upper-division undergraduates or delivers weekly lectures to hundreds attending introductory courses and confines its mentorship to supervising dissertations and theses. But in research universities, much of the real undergraduate teaching is done by the graduate assistants. Following the neoliberal economic doctrine that the labor policy of private and public sector employers should be to cut costs by reducing wages, by technological innovations such as online degree programs that can be taught by adjuncts, and by raising productivity (higher workloads, larger class sizes, and speed-up), educational administrators, disciplined by budget restraints, endeavor to cut the most expensive labor cost on campus: teachers. What better way to reduce costs, especially in Ivies and other elite schools where too many adjuncts tend to undermine the institution's claim to selectivity, than to stack graduate programs with students whose real function is bargain-basement labor? When a former president of the Modern Languages Association, Princeton Professor Elaine Showalter, suggested a draconian restriction on the production of doctorates, she was excoriated by the Left and the liberal academy. When Michael Berube and Cary Nelson, both respected English professors, argued for a two-tier graduate degree based on the distinction between research and teaching, they encountered similar rejection of their proposal that since most jobs are in institutions that mostly require teaching faculty, the PhD was unnecessary for many courses. Naturally, they wanted the second tier to be well paid and full time but would not expect teachers at that level to publish extensively in order to attain job security. On the other hand, their workloads would be higher than those of research university faculty. Some critics argued that the restriction was undemocratic and violated the precepts of an open society in which equality of opportunity was a cherished value. To confine the exalted perch of the doctorate to a select few, let alone relegating teaching to second-class status, was for many an unthinkable option, notwithstanding its effectiveness in maintaining the economic position of the professoriate. Yet Bosquet's argument that overproduction is a weapon in controlling the faculty—full as well as part time—remains powerful in the wake of chronic underfunding of higher education.

That such measures have not (yet) been imposed on K–12 is due, in part, to the failure of teacher unions to boldly oppose No Child Left Behind and other simplifying programs. But we cannot dismiss the steady drumbeat of neoliberal cost-cutting doctrine, or its consequences for the possibility of genuine education. Teachers' unions, already subordinated by the power of right-wing insistence on "standards"—a euphemism for the subordination of pedagogy to tests—will face a new and perhaps more insidious adversary. Unless and until unions, parents, and especially students are prepared to address the privatization and degradation of public education and the profound antilabor environment that pervades the field, the next step in federal and states' education policy is to emulate higher education in its relentless implementation of the casualization of teaching labor.

Ours is an era when, with the tacit approval of the education unions, disciplinary associations, students, and their families bear the skyrocketing costs of higher education. In many state institutions, they pay for 35 to 45 percent of instructional costs, and the percentage rises with every passing year. The absurd neoliberal idea that users should pay for every public good from parks and beaches to highways has reached higher education with a vengeance. This is a de facto privatization of public as much as private schooling—which has never refused public funds to meet its costs—even though governance remains in the hands of administrators, boards of trustees, and state legislators. At a moment when the values of collective action and organization are at a low ebb, and the neoliberal concept that the market should rule every human activity pervades public discourse, students and their families experience the institutions as they experience the state—remote, all-powerful, and punishing. And they have come to accept the notion that they, not the public sector, are ultimately responsible for any educational goods they are required to purchase. The key question is whether there is hope for a reversal in the near future, or whether a relatively few critics will continue to shout in the forest to the flora and the fauna but be ignored by any semblance of human forms.

The solution lies in the ability of critical educators to persuade their colleagues and their students that they are not fated to accept the given regime of educational degradation, that class sizes in many schools need to be reduced, that the fight to expand the number of full-time positions is a political struggle, and that they need collective forms of organization to win. Also needed is a conscious effort to bring teachers in higher education together with elementary and secondary school faculty in a common fight. This can be done by unions, but if they are recalcitrant, independent organizational forms may be needed to prod them. Without the will and the way to accomplish these tasks, there is no alternative but to expect a further diminution of school learning and a likely eclipse of the remnants of intellectual culture in the academy.

PART I
EDUCATION AND SOCIAL CLASS

◊

1

How Class Works in Education: A Memoir

I never knew my maternal grandmother. She died when my mother was twelve years old, an event that was to materially as well as psychologically shape my mother's life. When my grandfather remarried two years later, his new wife did not want my mother around, so she was sent to live with her father's sister, her husband, and her child. My mother's family—women as well as men—were garment workers. They came to the United States to escape the brutal czarist regime in Russia and Poland. Most of them were revolutionary socialists who were subject to imprisonment and exile. They were skilled workers who moved up the American class ladder—but without the benefit of school credentials. My grandfather was a highly skilled tailor who worked as a cutter in the men's clothing trade and eventually elevated himself to manage other workers. His sister Lily was a sewer of the whole garment in the high-end section of the dress industry. She sewed very expensive dresses by hand, a craft that has virtually disappeared except in the tiny custom dress market. Her husband, Zelig, began as a machine operator but became a writer and labor reporter for the *Jewish Daily Forward*, which, under the leadership of Abraham Cahan, its editor until World War II, was a real power among immigrant Jews. My grandmother's brother, a founder of a Cloak and Suit local of the International Ladies' Garment Workers' Union, was also a machine operator of ladies' coats and suits who, at the end of his life, became a small landlord with properties in the mostly black communities of the Bronx.

These were educated people who read and spoke several languages, who revered "classical" music but acquired their knowledge mostly in the course of their lives rather than in schools. Probably the one exception was that some of them attended union-sponsored citizenship classes in which they acquired knowledge of some U.S. history. And the union also ran English-language courses, using labor and socialist texts, novels, and daily newspapers. My great-uncle Zelig had a fairly large library of English- and Yiddish-language books in his home. I couldn't read the Yiddish, but the English-language books included contemporary works of American and European history, political commentary, and the novels of Dostoyevsky, Mann, and Kafka, among others. My mother attended high school in the Bronx until she was fourteen years old, but shortly after her mother died she was forced to drop out and go to work. She spent the next twenty-five years selling boys' clothing in several department stores and eventually became an assistant buyer at Klein's, one of the premier discount department stores in New York. For the more than twenty-five years before her retirement at age sixty-seven, she worked in union wholesale textile shops as an assistant bookkeeper. It was only after retirement that she fulfilled a lifelong aspiration to return to school, first earning her general equivalency diploma. She then started at a community college but left to attend the Center for Worker Education, a bachelor's degree program for union members and other working adults at City College of New York, where she graduated cum laude in 1987 at age seventy-four.

What my mother gained from schooling was no career but a bibliography and the chance to participate in discussions with fellow students about literature and politics, her two favorite subjects. She had been a voracious reader, musician, and painter throughout her life but, except for the arts, had never had the chance to share her literary insights with others. That, rather than career preparation, was the main value of school. Like her aunt and uncle, she was mostly self-taught except, perhaps, for her exquisite command of the English language, which, since Yiddish was the lingua franca of her parental and adopted households, probably required the drills that took place in PS 57 and Junior High School 45 in the Bronx.

I come from a family of unschooled but highly educated members of the "labor aristocracy." That is, most were highly skilled craftspersons who worked in factories or, in the case of my parents, as salaried employees. This advantage enabled them to live in neighborhoods that afforded more amenities than the communities dominated by semiskilled workers in mass production or service industries. And they were people who played musical instruments—my maternal grandfather played cello and violin, for example—read books, and were active in their respective unions. Their example, probably emulated unconsciously, prompted me to leave school in my freshman year of college, an event that upset both of my parents. But like them (my father did graduate from high school but left college after his first year), I felt that further schooling was superfluous to my intellectual development. Certainly after more than twelve years of schooling, I had come to the end of my tolerance for boredom and did not return to get a degree for fifteen years. It was only after I entertained the idea of leaving full-time union work—a job that required no advanced degrees—that I reentered undergraduate school on the condition that I would not be required to attend classes. My goal was to enter the life of writing and teaching, a vocation for which advanced degrees were necessary prerequisites. My sponsor, a professor at the New School, believed I could circumvent undergraduate schooling and move directly to graduate school. Placed in the charge of a mentor with whom I met once or twice during the academic year, I wrote a long paper and was duly certified as a bachelor of arts by the New School. In order to make this arrangement I agreed to attend the school's PhD program in sociology. After a stunning first semester sitting in classes taught by the likes of Jürgen Habermas, Iring Fetscher, and Adolph Lowe, I ran out of Germans and, faced with the prospect of studying with American sociologists schooled in the postwar shadow of Talcott Parsons and Robert Merton, the leading figures of a noncritical, positivist social science, I left school once more in the middle of the second semester and found a way to earn my PhD by other means, again without the obligation to take classes. Beginning with some observations in my first book, *False Promises,* for more than thirty years I have written about and commented on schooling, almost always in the context of considering the system from the vantage point of working-class students.

The Rocky Road to Educational Reform

My general disenchantment with schooling as we know it led me to participate in the founding of various types of alternative schools. The first, New York's Free University, was a non-degree-granting institution that was started by a group of radicals who believed that traditional schools had mostly ruined the passion for learning among young people who deserved another shot at a critical education. Founded in New York City in 1965, the school was one of a kind. In contrast to "socialist" schools of earlier and later vintage that were linked to specific political organizations and Marxist ideology, the Free University sought teachers with diverse knowledges and intellectual orientations who shared only a disdain for bureaucratic state institutions. The anarchist philosopher Murray Bookchin taught, as did the market libertarian and economist Murray Rothbard. The Marxian leftist James Weinstein, a historian and radical entrepreneur, was also a founder, and Alan Krebs, a defector from college teaching and later an ardent Maoist, whose inspiration it was to gather the original faculty and organizers, offered classes, as did the poet Susan Sherman. I taught there as well. Among my "students" were Robert Christgau and Ellen Willis, both in the process of inventing rock criticism, and Tuli Kupferberg, a member of the satirical singing group the Fugs. The school flourished in an environment of cultural revolution and political dissent that attracted people from literally all walks of life: workers, students, lawyers, physicians, artists, and, of course, Lower East Siders intent on reinventing the lost art of bohemianism. When the conditions that had produced the possibility of the school died—the protest movements of the 1960s, cheap rent, and relatively carefree youth—so did the Free University and all but a handful of its emulators.

Five years later I accepted a chance offered by a group of East Harlem and Yorkville parents to help organize an "experimental" public high school—the first since World War II—that would combine occupational and academic learning and be directed, primarily, toward working-class white, black, and Puerto Rican kids from East Harlem and Yorkville in Manhattan. Its planning phase was financed in part by the Ford Foundation, which was in the midst of its brief moment of fomenting educational innovations, and a reluctant New York City Board of Education. Park East High School opened in fall 1970 with 8 full-time teachers and 150 students drawn from both neighborhoods. Its first home was the basement of the local Catholic church; a nun from a local convent later joined the faculty, and other teachers, chosen by a committee of parents, were recruited from among licensed teachers credentialed by the board.

We began with no principal. Some of those duties were temporarily shared by the two full-time staff members responsible for organizing the school pending the selection of a licensed principal drawn from the official list. We had no problem with the requirement, imposed by the teachers' union—a representative of which sat on the governing committee—to hire from the official list because from a cohort of 20,000 high school teachers, we were bound to attract a handful of talented educators who really wanted to do something new. Selecting a principal from the approved list was another matter. In the first place, the pool of candidates was very small. More to the point, by the time a person attains high administrative rank, she or he has been a part of the system for decades, has learned its bureaucratic practices, and is likely to have internalized its values and intellectual orientation. We wanted a teacher/director, but the board and the supervisors' union would not hear of it. It turned out to be the eventual undoing of the school's aspiration to break away from the usual dismal character of nearly all state schools, especially the mostly dysfunctional high schools that littered New York City's neighborhoods.

Of course, the first two years were glorious. Student and teacher enjoyed a degree of freedom to invent new ways of learning. Consistent with the best work of developmental psychology, classroom practice was more than supplemented by extensive use of the vast resources of the city. For example, our biology teacher, who had studied at Indiana University with an eminent geneticist, was an ardent ecologist, so Central Park became a laboratory and our private bestiary. We commandeered a lab from a nearby hospital, and IBM donated a state-of-the-art computer lab that was in our own basement. Of course, the company had to send an instructor because none of the teachers or the administrators knew the first thing about computers. We all learned along with the students. Students were asked to suggest course electives and chose science fiction, Puerto Rican literature, the history of civil rights—and the staff scrambled to fulfill these desires. I taught the science fiction course to a class of twelve eager participants, and the course in Puerto Rican literature was taught by a neighborhood writer. For more than a few of the students, Park East was nothing short of a savior; years later a grateful parent met me at a Greenwich Village bar and refused to let me buy drinks. He claimed that I had saved his son from committing suicide. Others among the first cohort went on to become intellectuals, political activists, and top technical professionals. Thirty-five years later, I am still occasionally in touch with them.

Needless to say, this cornucopia came to an end with the arrival of the "real" principal, who convinced members of the governing committee—parents, community activists, and union officials—that the standard curriculum was best suited to ensure that students could gain access to colleges, a claim some of us disputed, but to little avail. Within a few years after my and my colleagues' departure (we had two- and three-year contracts to plan and execute the basic organization of the school but not to run it), Park East expanded to 600 students, acquired a real school building, and took its place among New York City high schools. It is still a relatively decent place but hardly the bastion of reform that it set out to be.

Although Park East was the first, it is by no means the last of small schools in New York and elsewhere. The most famous, Central Park East, founded by longtime school reformer Deborah Meier in the early 1980s, has succeeded in retaining much of its initial independence from the same old high school curriculum, but it has, inevitably, settled into a far less innovative space within New York's huge secondary school system. And of the dozens of exemplars of the small school movement that emerged on the heels of its success, several must be counted as relatively good places for kids. However, since 2001, when a new city administration took office and insisted on running the schools as a mayoral agency, school reform has fallen on hard times. The mania for endless testing that marks the Bush administration's No Child Left Behind program has been duplicated with a vengeance in New York City's high schools, and there are few exemptions. Although small may remain beautiful, and size matters for determining the degree of care that schools bestow on students, the impulse for reform has been crushed beneath the heavy boot of a banker turned school administrator who has made the mantra of "accountability" an excuse for racing backward to the nineteenth century. What we have learned from the tragic experience of the long struggle for school reform is that, like the New Deal's welfare state, nothing is forever. Neither in the United States nor almost anywhere else can we count on "progress" to secure popular gains that benefit working-class people. Just as the labor movement has entered into an era of full-scale retreat—a backward gallop that has witnessed the precipitous decline of real wages and benefits—so has schooling reverted to the preprogressive era in which, in the first place, black and Latino working-class kids are viewed as untamed beasts requiring constant surveillance by armed guards, a characterization that has not spared white kids either.

In late spring of 1972 I interviewed for a job at the Staten Island Community College (SICC) experimental school, a mélange of programs that had been encouraged by Bill Birenbaum, its president, as he later confessed, as his way of working around the largely vocational and professional emphasis of the rest of the institution. To accomplish this objective he needed to raise "soft" money—funds that were not provided by the city and state budgets. On the heels of the '60s penchant for doing new things, it was not too difficult to fund unconventional curricula. After a year of teaching in the experimental school my niche turned out to be a mandate to organize a "youth and community studies" associate's degree as a transfer to a parallel program at SUNY–Stony Brook, which offered a bachelor's degree in the subject. I was given a second teaching line to fill, and I hired David Nasaw, then a newly minted PhD in history from Columbia University. Nasaw was pleased to have the job at a time when history rivaled philosophy for the lack of full-time opportunities for even the products of the leading universities. We were foolish, so we took the program into three communities in addition to the SICC campus: Bedford-Stuyvesant, the Lower East Side, and Flatbush. We held classes in the storefronts and lofts of community organizations, which as late as the early '70s were still funded by city, state, and federal money. Our students were community outreach workers and, in the case of Flatbush, young adults who had had drug problems and wanted to go back to school. What courses we could not teach were handled by adjuncts, most of whom were people with extensive experience in community organizing and were eager to try their hand at classroom instruction.

Then came the New York City fiscal crisis of 1976 to the present, and with it a huge wet blanket descended over public education. That event signaled the end of the brief period of educational and other social reforms. It was the precursor of the so-called Reagan revolution, during which neoliberal policies—that is, privatized services—dominated public life. For the past thirty years we have been fed with a steady diet of market-driven concepts, the policy analog of which is that the private sector can do it better. The only new ideas that received any hearing were those having to do with cost cutting, administrative control of teachers and students, crime prevention, and the concept that schooling was about job preparation for private business. Government must now obey "bottom-line" criteria, as if any service were to be considered a commodity. Many professors and administrators still spouted the rhetoric of critical thinking and saw education as a preparation for "life," but as colleges and universities hired more adjuncts and fewer full-time teachers and workloads steadily increased, by the 1990s it became brutally apparent that the gulf between schooling and education had so widened that even the most cynical among us no longer denied that state schools had, for the most part, become credential mills. In many four-year as well as community colleges, corporations virtually seized the curriculum and instructors increasingly taught by the numbers; for example, in huge classes multiple-choice tests replaced the essay. All resistance to these self-evident rules had to go underground.

Go to College or Die

Ours is the era when "higher education" credentials have become the new mantra of public schooling. The rationale for the need for credentials is the technological imperative, the material basis of which is deindustrialization. The days when a teenager could drop out of high school and get a decent-paying factory job or go into retailing or wholesaling with a prospect of eventually earning enough to support self and family with dignity are, it seems, long gone. Now, we are told, from retailing to computer services and administration, everyone needs a degree. Whereas my family and I required none of the trappings of postsecondary schooling, today anyone possessing merely a high school diploma is consigned to low-wage jobs, or, if black or Latino, often no job at all.

But earning a degree does not an education make. On the contrary, as Peter McLaren and many others have noted, schooling is most often a ritual performance, both for the teacher and the student (McLaren 1999). For one thing, many kids leave high school without adequate preparation for college-level work. *College-level* here means the ability to perform research and write a long paper drawing on the relevant literature in the field. Although many upper-middle-class students have learned these "skills" already, most public high schools serving working-class students do not require serious academic performance as a criterion for graduation. At a time when politicians and their suppplicants sing the praises of science and mathematics as necessary prerequisites for technical jobs, many schools lack science laboratories or, if they have the space, do not supply up-to-date equipment so that students can perform even the most routine experiments in chemistry and biology. And systems are chronically short of qualified science and math teachers, the result of which is that many courses cannot be offered to meet entrance requirements of research universities and many private colleges. For another, as we have learned, environments for facilitating learning—books in the home, parents who can help teach their children how to use libraries, or even neighborhood libraries that have the materials and the staff to assist research—are not the norm. In short, in this richest and technologically most advanced society in the world, illiteracy in both its crude and its more sophisticated forms is rampant.

Ask any teacher working in a third-tier state or private college or university.[1] They normally have overcrowded classes of thirty-five or more, not only at the community colleges but at most of these institutions. In fact, some private colleges are the beneficiaries of students who have been refused admission to public colleges and universities where the pressure to maintain higher academic admission standards has reduced the number of working-class, especially black and Latino, students. In some cases middle-class whites are forced to seek private colleges because their high school records are simply not good enough for public schools. I know that this assertion seems counterfactual to the usual perception that the private schools are "better." This may be true of the 300 elite colleges and universities where class sizes are smaller and faculty members are always at students' disposal. But the third-tier story is quite different, at least in the Northeast, where these institutions are numerous. Of these students, many of my colleagues report that perhaps a fifth—seven or eight per class—are minimally prepared to address the tasks of the course, and far fewer are on top of the subject matter. Writing good papers is the exception even among these students. For most of my colleagues' classes, the ability of most students to read the assignments is in doubt. The quality of the students' oral class participation usually exceeds that of their written work, and when tests are required, the results are typically disheartening because, even when their reading is good enough, they have never been schooled in effective test-taking skills, let alone acquired the cultural capital their peers accumulate in private or upscale suburban public schools. Of course, given the fact that admissions offices still give more weight to the various scholastic "aptitude" tests than grade-point averages or recommendations, for upper-middle-class kids, attending a test-taking course given by a private tutorial company is de rigueur.

No doubt earning a postsecondary credential has become mandatory for the world of services and, in some cases, even for qualification for apprenticeships in union-sponsored highly skilled manual trades such as electrician and plumber. But as I have implied in this essay, the credential is incommensurate with the requirements of the job; its ubiquity is due chiefly to the widespread recognition that postsecondary credentials are absolutely necessary for qualification for the new world of work. And, except for the professions, the credential signifies not the necessary knowledge but the willingness of the student to submit to the controls that have been imposed by the chronic shortage of good-paying jobs.

In fact, we know that many graduates of elite schools feel impelled to seek a graduate degree because the bachelor's credential is widely regarded as merely a stepping-stone. The liberal arts graduate interested in the arts—writing, journalism, editing, film, or music composing or performance—is discovering the limits of his or her cultural capital. The once possible freelance career has almost vanished because many newspapers and magazines are gone, and online publications seldom offer a budding writer a way to make a living. Print media, including book publishing, are experiencing a sea change in their ability to stay alive. The entry-level job of assistant editor is disappearing as publishers pile more on harried editors; if there are editorial assistants, their pay is so low that they are likely to quit within the first year. And once-prosperous record companies that offered jobs to studio musicians, technicians, and entrepreneurial administrators are either folding or cutting their staffs to the bone. Aspiring filmmakers may have all the necessary skills and knowledge to make movies, but unless they go to a prestigious film school to earn a master's degree and acquire social capital—a fancy term for contacts and networks—they will find that their chance of catching on in any capacity within the industry, technical or artistic, is almost nil. Even the ambiguous title of management *trainee* often requires an MBA where once the bachelor's degree was sufficient. School systems and state agencies increasingly deny certification for elementary and secondary school teachers unless the master's degree has been presented. Teachers may be granted temporary credentials that permit them to teach but not to obtain tenure. And in the health professions, now the sector of choice for many working-class men as well as women because of the rapid growth of hospitals, nursing homes, and the key profession of nursing, where once an associate's degree was enough, now agencies and employers are requiring a minimum of a bachelor's degree in nursing and frequently make clear their preference for a master's degree. The poorly paid jobs in social work, especially in schools and medical institutions, have followed the credential inflation that marks most of the other subprofessions (jobs that do not require a PhD). As a consequence, hundreds of thousands of professionals are finding that their qualifications are outdated. Again, it's not that education schools and nursing schools, for example, offer "advanced" knowledge. It is simply a matter of control. Institutions want you to demonstrate your subordination by taking more and more courses and acquiring more credentials.

The class system in schooling has taken a new and disturbing turn. There is less education and more time spent in class. The vaunted American mobility system, always a partial truth, has all but collapsed. Students know that getting credentials is simply an endurance test, and most have no expectation of receiving a critical education. The problem is that in our profoundly anti-intellectual culture, it is hard to know where working-class young people can find an education. With the decline of the labor movement and the Left, once the best sources of critical thought, they are on their own, and until a real youth movement reemerges, the chances that things will change in this respect are dim. The unions resemble not so much a movement, for which the intellectual and political development as well as the interests of their members and the working class are paramount, as service organizations, best described as engaged in the business of survival. Their members are scarcely participants in the affairs of the union and do not and cannot expect to receive an alternative education. And the Left, disorganized and dispirited, is at best a mélange of single-issue movements and electoral machines for which the aspiration of providing an alternative education for its activists, let alone its potential constituents, is simply not on the agenda.

So where can a bright, intellectually ambitious young person turn? Perhaps inspiration and support come from the occasional teacher, perhaps from a fellow worker, perhaps from a chance encounter with ideas. What is certain is that in our profoundly anti-intellectual culture, on the whole they won't come from schools or the media. What is equally sure is that without an articulate and culturally motivated Left, the powerless will remain at the mercy of the system of control and subordination.

Notes

1. In my book *The Knowledge Factory* (Aronowitz 2000), I defined three tiers of the university system. The first is the handful of top research universities, including the Ivies; the Big Ten; the University of California; and major private schools such as Stanford, Chicago, and Duke. The second tier is the up-and-coming, not-yet-elite research universities of which New York University, Boston University, and Washington University are examples. The third tier is state and private four-year colleges, some of which have master's degree programs. In general, the elite private four-year colleges constitute a separate category: They may be "selective" schools but have virtually no institutional research agenda.

◇

2

Against Schooling:
Education and Social Class

The crisis in American education, on the one hand, announces the
bankruptcy of progressive education and, on the other hand, pre-
sents a problem of immense difficulty because it has arisen under
the conditions and in response to the demands of a mass society.
—*Hannah Arendt, 1961*

Americans have great expectations of their schools. We tend to
invest them with the primary responsibility for providing our
children with the means by which they may succeed in an increasingly uncertain work world. Moreover, if the child "fails" to
be inducted, through academic discipline, into the rituals of labor,
we blame teachers and school administrators. Indirectly, schools
have been burdened with addressing many of the world's ills.
Along with two world wars and various revolutions, the twentieth
century witnessed great hopes for democracy but experienced its
demise in the wake of the rise of many dictatorships. We knew
that education was the key to technological transformation, which
became the main engine of economic growth. Schooling was a
bulwark of secularism, but that function has buckled under the
onslaught produced by the revival of religious fundamentalism.
And in almost every economically "developed" country, we count
on schools to smooth the transition of huge populations from
rural to urban habitats, from "foreign" languages and cultures
to English and Americanism.

At the dawn of the new century, no American institution is
invested with a greater role in bringing the young and their
parents into the modernist regime than are public schools. The

common school is charged with the task of preparing children and youth for their dual responsibilities to the social order: citizenship and—perhaps its primary task—labor. On the one hand, in the older curriculum on the road to citizenship in a democratic, secular society, schools are supposed to transmit the jewels of the Enlightenment, especially literature and science. On the other, students are to be prepared for the work world by means of a loose but definite stress on the redemptive value of work; the importance of family; and, of course, the imperative of love and loyalty to one's country. Under the Enlightenment's concept of citizenship, students are, at least putatively, encouraged to engage in independent, critical thinking.

But the socializing functions of schooling play to the opposite idea: Children of the working and professional and middle classes are to be molded to the industrial and technological imperatives of contemporary society. Students learn science and mathematics not as a discourse of liberation from myth and religious superstition but as a series of algorithms, the mastery of which is presumed to improve the student's logical capacities, with no aim other than fulfilling academic requirements. In most places the social studies do not emphasize the choices between authoritarian and democratic forms of social organization, or democratic values, particularly criticism and renewal, but instead are disseminated as bits of information that have little significance for the conduct of life. Perhaps the teaching and learning of world literature in which some students are inspired by the power of the story to, in John Dewey's terms, "reconstruct" experience are a partial exception to the rule that for most students high school is endured rather than experienced as a series of exciting explorations of self and society (Dewey 1980).

Fiscal exigency and a changing mission have combined to leave public education in the United States in a chronic state of crisis. For some the main issue is whether schools are failing to transmit the general intellectual culture, even to the most able students. What is at stake in this critique is the fate of America as a civilization—particularly the condition of its democratic institutions and the citizens who are, in the final analysis, responsible for maintaining them. Hannah Arendt goes so far as to ask whether we "love the world" and our children enough to devise an educational system capable of transmitting the salient cultural traditions. Other critics complain that schools are failing to fulfill the promise to working-class students, black, Latino, and white, of equality of opportunity for good jobs. Although such critics are concerned with addressing the class bias of schooling, they unwittingly reinforce it by ignoring its content. The two positions, both with respect to their goals and to their implied educational philosophies, may not necessarily be contradictory, but their simultaneous enunciation produces considerable tension, for, with exceptions to be discussed later in this chapter, the American workplace has virtually no room for dissent and individual or collective initiative not sanctioned by management. The corporate factory, which includes sites of goods and symbolic production alike, is perhaps the nation's most authoritarian institution. But any reasonable concept of democratic citizenship requires an individual who is able to discern knowledge from propaganda, is competent to choose among conflicting claims and programs, and is capable of actively participating in the affairs of the polity. Yet the political system offers few opportunities, beyond the ritual of voting, for active citizen participation (Arendt 1961).

Even identifying the problem of why and how schools fail has proven to be controversial. For those who would define mass education as a form of training for the contemporary workplace, the problem can be traced to the crisis of authority—particularly school authority. That some of the same educational analysts favor a curriculum that stresses critical thinking for a small number of students in a restricted number of sites is consistent with the dominant trends of schooling since the turn of the twenty-first century. In its quest to restore authority, conservative educational policy has forcefully caused schools to abandon, both rhetorically and practically, the so-called child-centered curriculum and pedagogy. Instead, it favors a series of measures that not only hold students accountable for passing standardized tests and for a definite quantity of school knowledge (on penalty of being left back from promotion or expelled) but also impose performance-based criteria on administrators and teachers. For example, in New York City the schools chancellor has issued "report cards" to principals and has threatened to fire those whose schools do not meet standards established by high-stakes tests. These tests are the antithesis of critical thought. Their precise object is to evaluate the student's ability to imbibe and regurgitate information and to solve problems according to prescribed algorithms. A recent agreement between the New York City Department of Education and the teachers' union offers economic incentives to teachers whose students perform to preestablished testing standards, a sharp departure for a union that has traditionally contended that "merit"-pay schemes destroy solidarity.

On the other side, the progressives, who misread John Dewey's educational philosophy as meaning that the past need not be studied too seriously, have offered little resistance to the gradual vocationalizing and dumbing down of the mass education curriculum. In fact, historically they were advocates of making the curriculum less formal; reducing requirements; and, on the basis of a degraded argument that children learn best by "doing," promoting practical, work-oriented programs for high school students. Curricular deformalization was often justified on interdisciplinary criteria, which resulted in watering down course content and deemphasizing writing. Most American high school students, in the affluent as well as the "inner-city" districts, may write short papers, which amount to book reviews and autobiographical essays, but most graduate without ever having to perform research and write a paper of considerable length. Moreover, in an attempt to make the study of history more "relevant" to students' lives, since the late 1960s the student is no longer required to memorize dates; he may have learned the narratives but is often unable to place them in a specific chronological context. Similarly, economics has been eliminated in many schools or taught as a "unit" of a general social studies course. And if philosophy is taught at all, it is construed in terms of "values clarification," a kind of ethics in which the student is assisted in discovering and examining her own values.

That after more than a century of universal schooling the relationship between education and class has once more been thrust to the forefront is just one more signal of the crisis in American education. The educational Left, never strong on promoting intellectual knowledge as a substantive demand, clings to one of the crucial precepts of progressive educational philosophy: under the sign of egalitarianism, the idea that class deficits can be overcome by equalizing access to school opportunities without questioning what those opportunities have to do with genuine education. The access question has been in the forefront of higher-education debates since the early 1970s; even conservatives who favor vouchers and other forms of public funding for private and parochial schools have justified privatizing instruction on the grounds of access.

The structure of schooling already embodies the class system of society, and for this reason the access debate is mired in a web of misplaced concreteness. To gain entrance into schools always entails placement into that system. "Equality of opportunity" for class mobility is the system's tacit recognition that inequality is normative. In the system of mass education, schools are no longer constituted to transmit the Enlightenment intellectual traditions or the fundamental prerequisites of participatory citizenship, even for a substantial minority. Although acquiring credentials that are conferred by schools remains an important prerequisite for many occupations, the conflation of schooling with education is mistaken. Schooling is surely a source of training, both by its disciplinary regimen and its credentialing system. But schools do not transmit a "love for the world" or "for our children," as Arendt suggests; instead, contrary to their democratic pretensions, they teach conformity to the social, cultural, and occupational hierarchy. In our contemporary world, they are not constituted to foster independent thought, let alone encourage independence of thought and action. School knowledge is not the only source of education for students—perhaps not even the most important source.

On the contrary, in black and Latino working-class districts, schools are, for many students, way stations more to the military or to prison than to the civilian paid labor force. As Michelle Fine observes, "Visit a South Bronx high school these days and you'll find yourself surrounded by propaganda from the army/navy and marines. . . . Look at the 'stats' and you'll see that 70 percent of the men and women in prison have neither a GED nor a diploma; go to Ocean Hill–Brownsville 40ish years later, and you'll see a juvenile justice facility on the very site that they wanted to a build their own schools" (personal communication). In the current fiscal crisis afflicting education and other social services, there is an outstanding exception: Prisons continue to be well funded, and despite the decline of violent crimes in the cities, drug busts keep prisons full and rural communities working.

Young people learn, for ill as well as good, from popular culture, especially music; from parents and family structure; and, perhaps most important, from their peers. Schools are the stand-in for "society," the aggregation of individuals who, by contract or by coercion, are subject to governing authorities, in return for which they may be admitted into the world, albeit on the basis of different degrees of reward. To the extent that they signify solidarity and embody common dreams, popular culture, parents, and peers are the worlds of quasi-communities that are more powerful influences on their members.

Access to What?

In the main, the critique of education has been directed to the question of access, particularly in terms of the credentials that presumably open up the gates to higher learning or better jobs. Generally speaking, critical education analysis focuses on the degree to which schools are willing and able to open their doors to working-class students because, through their mechanisms of differential access, schools are viewed as, perhaps, the principal reproductive institutions of economically and technologically advanced capitalist societies. With some exceptions, most critics of schooling have paid scant attention to school authority; to the conditions for the accumulation of social capital—the intricate network of personal relations that articulate occupational access; or to cultural capital—the accumulation of the signs, if not the substance, of kinds of knowledge that are markers of distinction.

The progressives assume that the heart of the class question is whether schooling provides working-class kids with equality of opportunity to acquire legitimate knowledge and marketable academic credentials. They have adduced overwhelming evidence that contradicts schooling's reigning doctrine: that despite class, race, or gender hierarchies in the economic and political system, public education provides every individual with the tools to overcome conditions of birth. In reality, only about a quarter of people of working-class origin attain professional, technical, and managerial careers through the credentialing system. They find occupational niches, but not at the top of their respective domains. They typically graduate from third-tier, nonresearch colleges and universities, and their training does not entail acquiring the type of knowledge connected with substantial intellectual work: theory, extensive writing, and independent research. Students leaving these institutions find jobs as line supervisors, computer technicians, teachers, nurses, or social workers and in other niches in the social service professions.

A small number may join their better-educated colleagues in getting no-collar jobs, where "no-collar"—Andrew Ross's term—designates occupations that afford considerable work autonomy, such as computer design, which, although salaried, cannot be comfortably folded into the conventional division of manual and intellectual labor. The fact that so-called social mobility was a product of the specific conditions of American economic development at a particular time—the first quarter of the twentieth century—and was due principally to the absence of an indigenous peasantry during the U.S. industrial revolution and the forced confinement of millions of blacks to southern agricultural lands—is conveniently forgotten or ignored by consensus opinion. Nor do the celebrants of mobility take into account the labor shortages provoked by World War II and the subsequent U.S. dominance of world capitalism until 1973. Economic stagnation has afflicted the U.S. economy for more than three decades, and despite the well-known high-tech bubble of the 1990s, the U.S. economic position has deteriorated in the world market. Yet the mythology of mobility retains a powerful grip over the popular mind. The notion that schooling makes credentials available to anyone, regardless of rank or status, forms one of the sturdy pillars of American ideology (Ross 2003).

In recent years, the constitutional and legal assignment to the states and local communities of responsibility for public education has been undermined by what has been termed the "standards" movement, which is today the prevailing national educational policy, enforced not so much by federal law as by political and ideological coercion. At the state and district levels, the invocation to "tough love" has attained widespread support. We are witnessing the abrogation, both in practice and in rhetoric, of the tradition of social promotion whereby students moved through the system without acquiring academic skills. Having proven unable to provide to most working-class kids the necessary educational experiences that qualify them for academic promotion, more than a decade after its installation, the standards movement has revealed its underlying content: It is the latest means of exclusion, whose success depends on placing the onus for failure to achieve academic credentials on the individual rather than on the system. Although state departments of education frequently mandate that certain subjects be taught in every school and have established standards based on high-stakes tests applicable to all districts, everyone knows that districts with working-class majorities provide neither a curriculum and pedagogy nor facilities that meet these standards because, among other problems, they are chronically underfunded. But there is no shortage of money for the private corporations that are making huge profits on school systems.

High-stakes testing, a form of privatization, transfers huge amounts of public money to publishers, testing organizations, and large consulting companies. The state aid formulas, which, since the advent of conservative policy hegemony, have rewarded those districts whose students perform well on high-stakes standardized tests, tend to be unequal. Performance-based aid policies mean that school districts where the affluent live get more than their share and make up for state budget deficits by raising local property taxes and soliciting annual subventions from parents, measures not affordable by even the top layer of wage workers and low-level salaried employees. The result is overcrowded classrooms; poor facilities, especially laboratories and libraries; and underpaid, often poorly prepared teachers, an outcome of financially starved education schools in public universities.

Standards presuppose students' prior possession of cultural capital—an acquisition that almost invariably entails having been reared in a professional or otherwise upper-class family. In the main, even the most privileged elementary and secondary schools are ill equipped to compensate for home backgrounds in which reading and writing are virtually absent, a fact that has become a matter of indifference for school authorities. In this era of social Darwinism, poor school performance is likely to be coded as genetic deficit rather than being ascribed to social policy. Of course the idea that working-class kids, whatever their gender, race, or ethnic backgrounds, were selected by evolution or by God to perform material rather than immaterial labor is not new; this view is as old as class-divided societies. But in an epoch in which the chances of obtaining a good working-class job have sharply diminished, most kids face dire consequences if they don't acquire the skills needed in the world of immaterial labor. Not only are 75 percent assigned to working-class jobs but, in the absence of a shrinking pool of unionized industrial jobs, which often pay more than some professions such as teaching and social work, they must accept low-paying service sector employment, enter the informal economy, or join the ranks of the chronically unemployed.

From 1890 to 1920, the greatest period of social protest in American history before the industrial union upsurge of the 1930s, John Dewey, the leading educational philosopher of the progressive era, decisively transformed class discourse about education into a discourse of class leveling. Dewey's philosophy of education is a brilliant piece of bricolage: It combines an acute sensitivity to the prevailing inequalities in society with a pluralist theory, which by definition excludes class struggles as a strategy for achieving democracy. It was a feat that could have been achieved only by tapping into the prevailing radical critique of the limits of American democracy. But Dewey's aim was far from founding a new educational or political radicalism. True to the pragmatist tradition of "tinkering" rather than transforming institutions, Dewey sought to heal the breach between labor and capital through schooling. To the extent that schools afforded workers' children access to genuine education, American democracy—and the Americanization of waves of new immigrants—would be secure.

Dewey was not only America's preeminent philosopher, he was also a major intellectual spokesperson for the progressive movement at a time when social reform had achieved high visibility and had enormous influence over both legislation and public opinion, principally among wide sections of the middle class and in the higher circles of power. His writings helped bring education into the center of intellectual and political discourse by arguing that a society that wished to overcome the stigma of class distinction associated with industrial capitalism had to fervently embrace universal schooling. In addition, he was able to elaborate the doctrine that schooling was the heart of education, the core institution for the reproduction of liberal democratic society, and the basis for the objective of class leveling. In the end, "democracy in education" signifies that by means of universal schooling, all children, regardless of class origins, could have access to social mobility. Which is not egalitarian at all.

Democracy and Education (1916), Dewey's main philosophical statement on education, may be viewed in the context of the turn-of-the-twentieth-century emergence of mass public education, which, among other goals, was designed to address a multitude of problems that accompanied the advent of industrial society and the emergence of the United States as a world power. Among these problems were the enormous task of "Americanizing"—ideological education—millions of immigrants' children, most of whom were of the working class; the rise of scientifically based industrial and commercial technologies that, in the service of capital, required a certain level of verbal, scientific, and mathematical literacy among a substantial portion of the wage-labor force; the hard-won recognition by economic and political authorities as well as the labor movement that child labor had deleterious consequences for the future of the capitalist system; and, in an era of rapid technological change, the fact that industrial labor had become relatively expendable. In this context the high school became an important aging vat or warehouse, whether adolescents learned anything or not. As Michael B. Katz has shown, this concern was the basis of the public education movement in the nineteenth century because the question for educators, law enforcement officials, and political and economic leaders was what to do with unemployed youth during the day. The day prison was one solution, but Horace Mann prevailed upon his colleagues to establish public schools as a more "productive" way of containing unruly youngsters. Later the institution was expanded from six to twelve grades, and the minimum age for leaving rose from twelve to sixteen. After a century of compulsory secondary schooling, the educational value of high schools is still in doubt (Katz 1970).

At the outset, Dewey specifies the purposes of education: through adult transmission and communication, assisting the young to direct their own lives. Dewey cautions that because the young hold society's future in their hands, the nature of adults' transmissions inevitably has serious consequences. Yet, having recognized, briefly, the role of "informal" education in the self-formation of the young, Dewey establishes the rule for virtually all subsequent educational philosophy. Consistent with a liberal democratic society, he exhorts educators to devise a formal method for directing the future: by organization of a common *school* that provides the necessary discipline, array of learning, and methods by which learning that reproduces the social order may occur. Although transmitting and communicating knowledge are intended to provide "meaning to experience," and Dewey invokes "democratic criteria" as the basis for his concept of the "reconstruction of experience," the objective of "control and growth" in order to achieve "social continuity" occupies an equally important place in any enterprise that seeks to explore the creative possibilities of education (Dewey 1980, 331).

Dewey walks a tightrope between the creative side of education as a playful and imaginative reflection on experience and the necessary task of reproducing the social order, in which work, albeit as much as possible creative, remains the key educational goal. But he also endorses the role of the school in training the labor force. Dewey advocates for the ability of children to obtain the knowledge that could aid in their quest for an autonomous future even as he approaches the problem of moral education (character building, values) from the perspective of society's need to reproduce itself on the basis of the criteria inherited from the past. He deplores the separation of labor and leisure, the cleavage of liberal arts and vocational education in which the former is regarded as activity to be tolerated but not enjoyed. Labor should be viewed not as a "job" but rather, as much as possible, as a "calling." Without addressing the nature of the rationalized labor to which wage workers, including most professional and technical workers, are subjected, Dewey's educational philosophy is directed mostly to the ideal of educational humanism. Class distinctions are not denied but are assumed to be blurred, if not eliminated, by democratic education.

In both their critical and celebratory variants of his philosophy, Dewey's intellectual children, with few exceptions, have not addressed the issue of whether, given their conflictual purposes and hierarchical organization, schools can fulfill their liberal democratic, let alone egalitarian, promise. Having narrowly confined itself to school practices, post-Deweyan progressive educational thought has recoded Dewey's philosophy by invoking phrases such as "self-realization" and "child-centered" to describe education's goals. Or, worse, Dewey has been used to justify a relentless instrumentalism in curriculum design: In the name of antitraditionalism and nationalism, high schools do not teach philosophy or social history—principally the role of social movements in making history—or treat world literature as a legitimate object of academic study. Needless to say, few if any critics have challenged the curricular exclusions of working-class history, let alone the histories of women and of blacks. Nor have curricular critics addressed the exclusion of philosophy and social theory.

In recent years the philosophy of education has waned and been replaced by a series of policy-oriented empirical research projects that conflate democracy with access and openly subordinate school knowledge to the priorities of the state and the corporations. Educational thought has lost, even renounced, Dewey's program directed to the reconstruction of experience. In fact, after the early grades, student experience is viewed by many educators and administrators with suspicion, even hostility. Recent educational policy has veered toward delineating preschool and kindergarten as sites for academic and vocational preparation. If the child is to grow to become a productive member of society—where productive is equated with work-ready—play must be directed, free time severely constrained. The message emanating from school authorities is to "forget" all other forms and sites of learning. Academic and technical knowledge become the only legitimate forms, and the school is the only reliable site. Whatever their defects, in contrast with the penchant of modern educational researchers for focusing on "policy" to the detriment of historical and theoretical analysis, Dewey's ideas demonstrate a passion for citizenship and ambivalence about the subordination of education to the imperatives of the system. He deplored the subordination of knowledge to the priorities of the state while, at the same time, extolling the virtues of the liberal state, and he subjected vocational education to the scrutiny of the Enlightenment prescription that education be critical of the existing state of affairs while at the same time approving the reproductive function of schools.

The rise of higher education since World War II has been seen by many as a repudiation of academic elitism. Do not the booming higher-education enrollments validate the propositions of social mobility and democratic education? Not at all. Rather than constituting a sign of rising qualifications and widening opportunity, burgeoning college and university enrollments signify changing economic and political trends. The scientific and technical nature of our production and service sectors increasingly requires qualified and credentialed workers (it would be a mistake to regard those two things as identical). Students who would have sought good factory jobs in the past now believe, with reason, that they need credentials to qualify for a well-paying job. On the other hand, even as politicians and educators decry social promotion and most high schools with working-class constituencies remain aging vats, mass higher education is, to a great extent, a holding pen because it effectively masks unemployment and underemployment. This function may account for its rapid expansion over the past thirty-five years of chronic economic stagnation, deindustrialization, and proliferation of part-time and temporary jobs, largely in the low-paid service sectors. Consequently, working-class students are able, even encouraged, to enter universities and colleges at the bottom of the academic hierarchy—community colleges but also public four-year colleges—thus fulfilling the formal pledge of equal opportunity for class mobility even as most of these institutions suppress the pledge's content. But grade-point averages, which in the standards era depend as much as the Scholastic Aptitude Test on high-stakes testing, measure the student's acquired knowledge and restrict her access to elite institutions of higher learning, the obligatory training grounds for professional and managerial occupations. Because all credentials are not equal, graduating from third- and fourth-tier institutions does not confer on the successful candidate the prerequisites for entering a leading graduate school—the preparatory institution for professional or managerial occupations—or for the most desirable entry-level service jobs that require only a bachelor's degree (Aronowitz 2000).

Pierre Bourdieu argues that schools reproduce class relations by reinforcing rather than reducing class-based differential access to social and cultural capital, key markers of class affiliation and mobility. These forms of capital, he argues, are always already possessed by children of the wealthy, professionals, and the intelligentsia. Far from making possible a rich intellectual education or providing the chance to affiliate with networks of students and faculty who have handles on better jobs, schooling uses mechanisms of discipline and punishment to habituate working-class students to the bottom rungs of the work world, or the academic world, by subordinating or expelling them (Bourdieu and Passeron 1977). Poorly prepared for academic work by their primary and secondary schools, and having few alternatives to acquiring some kind of credential, many who stay the course and graduate high school and third- and fourth-tier colleges inevitably confront a series of severely limited occupational choices—or none at all. Their life chances are just a cut above those of the students who do not complete high school or college. Their school performances seem to validate what common sense has always suspected: Given equal opportunity to attain school knowledge, the cream always rises to the top, and those stuck at the bottom must be biologically impaired or victimized by the infamous "culture of poverty." The fact that most working-class high school and college students are obliged to hold full- or part-time jobs in order to stay in school fails to temper this judgment, for, as is well known, preconceptions usually trump facts (Cicourel and Kitrae 1963). Nor does the fact that children of the recent 20 million immigrants from Latin America and Asia speak their native languages at home, in the neighborhood, and to each other in school evoke more than hand-wringing from educational leaders; in this era of tight school budgets, funds for teaching English as a second language have been cut or eliminated at every level of schooling.

But Paul Willis insists that working-class kids get working-class jobs by means of their refusal to accept the discipline entailed in curricular mastery and by their rebellion against school authority. Challenging the familiar "socialization" thesis, of which Bourdieu's is perhaps the most sophisticated version, according to which working-class kids "fail" because they are culturally deprived—or, in the American critical version, are assaulted by the hidden curriculum and school pedagogy, which subsumes kids under the prevailing order—Willis recodes kids' failure as refusal of (school) work (Willis 1981). This refusal lands them in the factory or low-level service jobs. Willis offers no alternative educational model to schooling: His discovery functions as critique. Indeed, as Willis himself acknowledges, the school remains, in Louis Althusser's famous phrase, the main "ideological state apparatus," but working-class kids are not victims. Implicitly rejecting Sennett and Cobb's notion that school failure is a "hidden injury" of class insofar as working-class kids internalize poor school performance as a sign of personal deficit, he argues that most early school leavers are active agents in the production of their own class position (Althusser 1971; Sennett and Cobb 1973). Although students' antipathy to school authority is enacted at the site of the school, its origin is the working-class culture from which it springs. Workers do not like bosses, and kids do not like school bosses, the deans and principals, but often the teachers as well, whose main job in the urban centers is to keep order. The source of working-class kids' education is not the school but the shop floor where their parents work, the home, and the neighborhood. I'll discuss this concept in more detail later in this chapter.

In the past half century the class question has been inflected by race and gender discrimination, and, in the American way, the "race, gender, class" phrase implies that these domains are ontologically distinct, if not entirely separate. Many educational theorists have conceived of the race and gender question not as a class issue but as an attribute of biological identities. In fact, in the era of identity politics, class itself stands alongside race and gender as just another identity. Having made the easy, inaccurate judgment that white students, regardless of their class or gender, stand in a qualitatively different relation to school-related opportunities than blacks, these theorists often suppress the notion of class as a sign of exclusion. In privileging issues of access, not only is the curriculum presupposed, in which case Bourdieu's insistence on the concept of cultural capital is ignored, but also the entire question of whether schooling may be conflated with education is elided. Only rarely do writers examine other forms of education. In both the Marxist and the liberal tradition, schooling is presumed to remain, over a vast spectrum of spatial and temporal situations, the theater within which life chances are determined.

Education and Immaterial Labor

Education may be defined as the collective and individual reflection on the totality of life experiences: what we learn from peers, parents and the socially situated cultures of which they are a part, media, and schools. By "reflection" I mean the transformation of experience into a multitude of concepts that constitute the abstractions we call "knowledge." Which of the forms of learning predominate is always configured historically. The exclusive focus by theorists and researchers on school knowledge—indeed, the implication that school is the principal site of what we mean by education—reflects the degree to which they have internalized the equation of education with school knowledge and its preconditions. The key learning is to habituate students to a specific regimen of intellectual labor that entails a high level of self-discipline, the acquisition of the skills of reading and writing, and the career expectations associated with professionalization.

To say this constitutes the self-reflection by intellectuals—in the broadest sense of the term—of their own relation to schooling. In the age of the decline of critical intelligence and the proliferation of technical intelligence, "intellectual" in its current connotation designates immaterial labor rather than those engaged in traditional intellectual pursuits such as literature, philosophy, and art. Immaterial labor describes those who work not with objects or administration of things and people but with ideas, symbols, and signs. Some of the occupations grouped under immaterial labor have an affective dimension, particularly people who, in one way or another, care for each other. Such work demands the complete subordination of brain, emotion, and body to the task while requiring the worker to exercise considerable judgment and imagination in its performance (Hardt and Negri 1994). At sites such as "new economy" private-sector software workplaces; some law firms that deal with questions of intellectual property, public interest, constitutional, and international law; research universities and independent research institutes; and small, innovative design, architectural, and engineering firms, the informality of the labor process, close collaborative relationships among members of task-oriented teams, and the overflow of the space of the shop floor into the spaces of home and play can evoke a high level of exhilaration, even giddiness, among workers (Ross 2003). But such relationships are also present in such work as teaching; child care; care for seniors; and the whole array of therapeutic services, including psychotherapy.

Immaterial workers, in the interest of having self-generated work, surrender much of their unfettered time. They are obliged to sunder the conventional separation of work and leisure, to adopt the view that time devoted to creative, albeit commodified, labor is actually "free." To be more exact, even play must be engaged in as serious business. For many, the golf course, the bar, the weekend at the beach are workplaces in which dreams are shared, plans formulated, and deals made. Just as time becomes unified around work, so work loses its geographic specificity. As Andrew Ross shows in his pathbreaking ethnography of a New York new economy workplace during and after the dot.com boom, the headiness for the pioneers of this new work world was, tacitly, a function of the halcyon period of the computer software industry when everyone felt the sky was no longer the limit. When the economic crunch descended on thousands of workplaces, people were laid off, and those who remained experienced a heavy dose of market reality.

It may be argued that among elite students and institutions, not only does schooling prepare students for immaterial labor by transmitting a bundle of legitimate knowledge, but the diligent, academically successful student internalizes the blur between the classroom, play, and the home by spending a great deal of time in the library or ostensibly playing at the computer. Thus, the price of the promise of autonomy, a situation that is intrinsic to professional ideology, if not always its practice in the context of bureaucratic and hierarchical corporate systems, is to accept work as a mode of life: One lives to work, rather than the reverse. The hopes and expectations of people in these strata are formed in the process of schooling; indeed, they are the ones who most completely assimilate the ideologies linked to school knowledge and to the credentials conferred by the system. Thus, even if they are not professional school people or educational researchers, they tend to evaluate people by the criteria to which they themselves were subjected. If the child has not fully embraced work as life, he is consigned to the educational netherworld. Even the egalitarians (better read as populists) accept this regime: Their object is to indoctrinate those for whom work is a necessary evil into the social world where work is the mission.

Media and Popular Culture

Most educators and critics acknowledge the enormous role of media in contemporary life. The ubiquity and penetration of visual media such as TV, VCR and DVD players, videogames, and electronic sound equipment such as CD and tape players into the home has called into question the separation of the public and private spheres and challenged the notion that autonomous private life any longer exists. Writers such as Hannah Arendt insist on the importance of maintaining the separation of the two spheres (Arendt 1958). When taken together with the advent, in the technical as well as metaphoric sense, of "big brother"—with the government now openly announcing its intention to subject every telephone and computer to surveillance—it is difficult to avoid the conclusion that media are a crucial source of education and may, in comparison to schools, exercise a greater influence on children and youth. Many claim that television, for example, is the prime source of political education, certainly the major source of news, for perhaps a majority of the population. And there is a growing academic discourse on the importance of popular culture, especially music and film, in shaping the values, but more to the point the cultural imagination, of children and adolescents. Many writers have noted the influence of media images on children's dream work; on their aspirations; on their measurement of self-worth, both physical and emotional. Of course debate rages as to what is learned—for example, the implied frameworks that are masked by the face of objectivity presented by television news and by fiction, which, as everybody knows, is suffused with ethical perspective on everyday relations (Horkheimer and Adorno 2002; Macdonald 1983; McLuhan 1964).

Nor does every critic accept the conventional wisdom that, in the wake of the dominance of visual media in everyday life, we are, in the phrase of a leading commentator, "amusing ourselves to death," or that the ideological messages of popular music, sitcoms, and other TV fare are simply conformist (Postman 1986). But it must be admitted that since the 1920s and 1930s, when critics argued that the possibility of a radical democracy in which ordinary people participated in the great and small decisions affecting their lives was undermined by the advent of the culture industry, popular culture has to a large degree become a weapon against, as well as for, the people. As a general rule, in periods of upsurge—when social movements succeed in transforming aspects of everyday life as well as the political landscape—art, in its "high" as well as popular genres, expresses a popular yearning for a better world. In this vein, a vast literature, written largely by participants in the popular culture since the 1960s, rejects the sharp divide between high and low art. Many contemporary cultural critics such as Greil Marcus and Robert Christgau acknowledge their debt to the work of the critical theory of the Frankfurt School, particularly that of Herbert Marcuse and Theodor Adorno, owing both to their independent judgment and to the influence of Walter Benjamin—who, despite his elective affinity to critical theory, welcomed, with some trepidation, the eclipse of high art. However, these same critics find a subversive dimension in rock-and-roll music (Christgau 2001; Marcus 1975). It may be that the 1960s phrase "sex, drugs, and rock 'n' roll" no longer resonates as a universal sign of rebellion. Yet, when evaluated from the perspective of a society that remains obsessed with drug use and premarital sex among youth and "blames" the music for kids' nonconformity, the competition between school and popular culture still rages. From anthems of rebellion to musical expressions of youth rejection of conventional sexual and political morality, critics have detected signs of resistance to official mores.

Of course even as punk signaled the conclusion of a sort of "golden age" of rock and roll and the succeeding genres—heavy metal, alternative, and techno, among others—were confined to market niches, hip-hop took on some of the trappings of a universal oppositional cultural form and by the 1990s had captured the imagination of white as well as black kids. Out of the "bonfires" of the Bronx came a new generation of artists whose music and poetry enflamed the embers of discontent. Figures such as Ice-T, Tupac Shakur, Biggie Small, and many others articulated the still vibrant rebellion against what George Bernard Shaw once called "middle class morality" and the smug, suburban confidence that the cities could be safely consigned to the margins. Like Dylan, some of the hip-hop artists were superb poets: Tupac had many imitators, and eventually the genre became fully absorbed by the culture industry, a development that, like the advent of the Velvets, the Who, and other avant-garde rock groups of the early 1970s, gave rise to an underground. And, just as rock-and-roll musicians were accused of leading young people astray into the dungeons of drugs and illicit sex, the proponents of hip-hop suffered a similar fate. Some record producers succumbed to demands that they censor artistic material; radio stations refused to air some hip-hop songs; and record stores, especially in suburban malls, were advised to restrict sales of certain artists and records.

What white kids have learned from successive waves of rock and roll and hip-hop music is chiefly their right to defy ordinary conventions. After the mid-1950s, the varied genres of rock, rhythm and blues, and hip-hop steadily challenged the class, racial, and sexual constructs of this ostensibly egalitarian but puritanical culture. Bored and dissatisfied with middle-class morality and its cultural values, teenagers flooded the concerts of rock and hip-hop stars, smoked dope, and violated the precepts of conventional sexual morality to the best of their abilities. Many adopt black rhetoric, language, and disdain for mainstream values. Of course middle-class kids are obliged to lead a double life because their preferred artistic and cultural forms are accorded absolutely no recognition in the world of legitimate school knowledge. Also, for reasons I have already stated, they are in a double bind: Since the 1960s their shared music and the messages of rebellion against a racist, conventional, suburban, middle-class culture have constituted a quasi-countercommunity. Yet, on penalty of proscription, they must absorb school knowledge without invoking the counterknowledge of popular culture.

The products of visual culture, particularly film and television, are no less powerful sources of knowledge. Since movies became a leading form of recreation early in the twentieth century, critics have distinguished schlock from "films" produced both by the Hollywood system and by a beleaguered corps of independent filmmakers. In the 1920s, elaborating the dynamic film technique pioneered by D. W. Griffith, the Soviet filmmakers, notably Sergei Eisenstein and Zhiga Vertov, and the great cultural critic Siegfried Kracauer fully comprehended the power of visual culture in its ornamental, aesthetic sense, and gave pride of place to film as a source of mass education. Vertov's *Man with a Movie Camera* and Eisenstein's *October* were not only great works of art, they also possessed enormous didactic power (Kracauer 1995). Vertov evoked the romance of industrial reconstruction in the new Soviet regime and the imperative of popular participation in building a new technologically directed social reality. And in most of his films, Eisenstein was the master of revolutionary memory: The people should not forget how brutal was the ancient regime and that the future was in their hands, and he would produce the images that created a new "memory" even among those who had never experienced the heady days of the revolution. Of course Griffith conveyed a different kind of memory: In his classic *Birth of a Nation*, he deconstructed the nobility and romance of the U.S. Civil War and the Reconstruction period by depicting those events as a corrupt alliance of blacks and northern carpetbaggers, the epithet applied to the staff of the Freedmen's Bureau and the military who were dispatched to guarantee the newly won civil rights of millions of African Americans.

In 1950 anthropologist Hortense Powdermaker termed Hollywood "the dream factory." Although we were entertained by the movies, she argued, a whole world of hopes and dreams was being manufactured that had profound effects on our collective unconscious. Rather than coding these experiences as "illusion," she accorded them genuine social influence. With the later writings of critics André Bazin, François Truffaut, Christian Metz, Stephen Heath, Laura Mulvey, and Pauline Kael, movies came into their own as an art form but also as a massive influence on what we know and how we learn. Film, which for critical theory was just another product of the culture industry, is now taken seriously by several generations of critics and enthusiasts as a many-sided cultural force. At the same time, film criticism has evolved from reviews in the daily and weekly press and television (whose main function is to advise the public whether to choose a particular film or to hire a babysitter to attend a movie) into a historical and critical discipline worthy of academic departments and programs, and whose practitioners are eligible for academic rank (Bazin 1989; Metz 1991; Kael 1994; Powdermaker 1950).

Despite their ubiquity and vast influence, the kinds of knowledge derived from mass media and popular music remain largely unexamined by the secondary school curriculum. In this respect, public education may be regarded as one of the last bastions of high cultural convention and of the book. Perhaps more to the point, by consistently refusing to treat popular culture—television, film, music, and video games—as objects of legitimate intellectual knowledge, schools deny the validity of student experiences, even if the objective were to deconstruct them. Thus, a century after mass-mediated music and visual arts captured our collective imagination, popular culture remains subversive, notwithstanding its undeniable commodification and regardless of its content, because it continues to be outlawed in official precincts. By failing to address this epochal phenomenon, even as its forms are overwhelmingly influential in everyday life, school knowledge loses its capacity to capture the hearts and minds of its main constituents. And if schools cannot enter the students' collective imagination, other forms of knowledge are destined to fill the vacuum.

Of course the power of television in shaping the political culture is far less well understood. If the overwhelming majority of the population receives its news and viewpoints from television sources, then, without such counterweights as those that may be provided by social movements, counterhegemonic intellectuals, and independent media, the people are inevitably subjected to the ruling common sense. Alternatives to the official stories lack legitimacy, even when they are reported in the back pages or in a thirty-second spot on the 11 o'clock news. Even journalists have discovered that the integration of major news organizations with the ruling circles inhibits their ability to accurately report the news. For example, on October 26, 2002, more than 100,000 people descended on Washington, D.C., to protest the Bush administration's plan to wage war against Iraq. The *New York Times* reporter on the scene estimated the crowd in the "thousands" and stated that the turnout had disappointed organizers, who had expected more than 100,000 demonstrators to show up. Since the *Times* functions as a guide to the rest of the American news media, including television and radio news, the coverage of the demonstration throughout the nation was scanty, in part because other media relied on the *Times*'s understated numbers. For the majority of Americans, the original report and its numerous recapitulations left the impression that the demonstration was a bust. But the *Washington Post,* perhaps the *Times*'s only competitor in daily print journalism, estimated the number of demonstrators more or less accurately, and by the evening of the event a wealth of information and furious condemnation of the *Times*'s biased coverage had swarmed over the Internet. Days later, in an obscure little piece, the paper's editors issued a correction without referring the readers to the previous report.

But more importantly, the relation of education and class is indicated by the way in which issues are framed by experts, opinion surveys, and the media, which faithfully feature them. That Iraq's president, Saddam Hussein, and his government constituted an imminent threat to U.S. security—a judgment for which neither the media nor the Bush administration seemed to require proof—was the starting point of virtually all of the media's coverage of U.S. foreign policy during the first years of the U.S. war on Iraq. On the nightly news or the Public Broadcasting System's (PBS's) many programs of talking expert heads, no less than on Sunday-morning talk shows on commercial networks in which experts mingle with the political directorate to discuss world and national events, the question of whether there is warrant for this evaluation was almost never posed. Instead, discussion revolved around the issue not of *whether* the United States should go to war to disarm the Iraqi regime but of *when* the invasion would inevitably occur. The taken-for-granted assumption was that Saddam had viable "weapons of mass destruction" in his possession, whether or not the United Nations inspectors dispatched by the Security Council to investigate this allegation could affirm this U.S. government–manufactured "fact." Since the Bush administration knew that there was nothing as efficient as a war to unify the underlying population behind its policies, and the media were complicit, citizens were deprived of countervailing assessments unless they emanated from within the establishment. And even then, there was only a small chance that these views would play prominently.

Thus, when Brent Scowcroft, the national security adviser in the first Bush administration, and retiring Republican conservative U.S. Representative Dick Armey expressed reservations about the current administration's war plans, neither received the notice that such an ideological breach might deserve. Only the tiny fraction of the population that reads a handful of liberal newspapers and opinion magazines were likely to know about their objections. From the perspective of the leading media, Americans (except for African Americans) were, in the months leading up to the U.S. invasion, in virtual unanimous agreement that we should and would go to war against Iraq. Yet, according to the results of some polls that were poorly reported in most media, we know that support for the war was not only soft but was qualified; whereas few were opposed to a war on any terms, many Americans objected to a unilateral attack by U.S. forces, a belief that was partially responsible for the administration's formation of a "coalition" to undertake the tasks of invasion and occupation. But there were ample indications that the administration proceeded *as if* public opinion were unified around its policy. In this mode of governance, absent massive protest that might manifest directly or electorally, silence is tantamount to consent. Without visible dissent—a visibility routinely denied by the media to protestors—the administration interpreted the Republican victory in the 2002 midterm elections as a retrospective mandate for its war policies.

The pattern of government vetting and censorship of war news was established during World War II, but the first Bush administration elevated it to an art form. During the 1991 Gulf War, the administration took pains to shield reporters from the battlefield and insisted that they be quartered in Saudi hotels, miles away from the action. Journalists received all of the war news from government sources, including video footage and photographs shown to them in special briefings. According to the contemporary and subsequent testimony of some journalists who were assigned to cover the events, the Bush administration was intent on not repeating the mistakes of the Vietnam War, when the Johnson administration permitted the press full access to American and enemy troops and to the battle scenes. Historians and political observers agree that this policy may have had a major impact on building the antiwar movement—especially the images of body bags being loaded onto airplanes and the human gore associated with any close combat supplied by staff photographers. In 1991 Americans never got the chance to view the physical and human destruction visited by U.S. bombs and missiles on Baghdad or the extent of U.S. casualties. The war was short-lived, so the political damage at home was relatively light. Needless to say, the fact that some 150,000 of the 700,000 troops who entered the combat area have since reported psychological or physical injuries barely makes it to the back pages of most newspapers, let alone the visual media.

Note well that at its inception, some educators and producers touted the educational value of television. Indeed, perhaps the major impact of the dominance of visual culture on our everyday knowledge is that to be is to be seen. "Celebrity" is a word reserved for people whose names become "household" words. Celebrity is produced by the repetition of appearances of an individual on the multitude of television talk shows—the *Oprah Winfrey Show*, the *Today Show*, Jay Leno's *Tonight Show*, and the *Late Show with David Letterman*, among others—in which personalities constitute the substance of the event. The point of the typical interview between the anchor and her or his subject is not what is said, or even that the guest is currently appearing in a film or television show, the ostensible purpose of the segment. The interview is a statement of who exists and, by implication, who doesn't. The event has little to do with economic or high-level political power, for these people are largely invisible, or on occasion may appear on the *Charlie Rose Show* on PBS or, formerly, on ABC's *Nightline*. The making of sports, entertainment, political, or literary celebrities defines the boundary of popular hope or aspiration. The leading television celebrity talk shows are instances of the American credo that, however high the barrier, anyone can become a star. This is not an instance of having charisma or exuding aura: The celebs are not larger than life but are shown to be ordinary in an almost banal sense. Fix your nose, cap your teeth, lose weight, take acting lessons, and, with a little luck, the person on the screen could be you.

The Labor and Radical Movements as Educational Sites

The working-class intellectual as a social type precedes and parallels the emergence of universal public education. At the dawn of the public school movement in the 1830s, the antebellum labor movement, which consisted largely of literate skilled workers, favored six years of schooling in order to transmit to children the basics of reading and writing but opposed compulsory attendance in secondary schools. The reasons were bound up with the movement's congenital suspicion of the state, which it believed never exhibited sympathy for the workers' cause. Although opposed to child labor, the early workers' movement was convinced that the substance of education—literature, history, philosophy—should be supplied by the movement itself. Consequently, in both the oral and the written tradition, workers' organizations often constituted an alternative university to that of public schools. The active program of many workers' and radical movements until World War II consisted largely in education through newspapers, literacy classes for immigrants in which the reading materials were drawn from labor and socialist classics, and world literature. These were supplemented by lectures offered by independent scholars who toured the country in the employ of lecture organizations commissioned by the unions and radical organizations (Teitelbaum 1995).

The shop floor was also a site of education. Skilled workers were usually literate in their own language and in English, and many were voracious readers and writers. Union and radical newspapers often printed poetry and stories written by workers. Socialist-led unions such as those in the needle, machinist, brewery, and bakery trades sponsored educational programs; in the era when the union contract was still a rarity, the union was not so much an agency of contract negotiation and enforcement as an educational, political, and social association. In his autobiography, Samuel Gompers, the founding president of the American Federation of Labor, remembers his fellow cigar-makers in the 1870s hiring a "reader" who sat at the center of the work floor and read from literary and historical classics as well as more contemporary works of political and economic analysis such as the writings of Marx and Engels. Reading groups met in the backs of bars, in union halls, or in the offices of local affiliates of socialist wings of nationality federations. Often these groups were ostensibly devoted to preparing immigrants to pass the obligatory language test for citizenship status. But reading, in addition to labor and socialist newspapers and magazines, was often supplemented by works by Shakespeare, the great nineteenth-century novelists and poets, and Marx and Karl Kautsky. In the anarchist incarnation of these readings, Pyotr Kropotkin, Moses Hess, and Mikhail Bakunin were the required texts (Gompers 1924).

In New York, Chicago, San Francisco, and other large cities where the socialist and communist movements had considerable membership and a fairly substantial periphery of sympathizers, the parties established adult schools that not only offered courses pertaining to political and ideological knowledge but were also vehicles for many working- and middle-class students to gain a general education. Among them, in New York the socialist-oriented Rand School and the communist-sponsored Jefferson School (formerly the Workers' School) lasted until the early 1950s, when, owing to the decline of a leftist intellectual culture among workers as much as the repressive political environment, they closed. But in their respective heydays, from the 1920s to the late 1940s, for tens of thousands of working-class people—many of them high school students and industrial workers—these schools were alternative universities. They didn't offer only courses that promoted the party's ideology and program; many courses concerned history, literature, and philosophy, and—at least at the Jefferson school—students could also study art, drama, and music, and so could their children. The tradition was revived briefly by the 1960s New Left, which sponsored free universities for which the term "free" designated not an absence of tuition but the fact that the schools were ideologically and intellectually unbound to either the traditional Left parties or the conventional school system. I participated in organizing New York's Free University and two of its successors. Although not affiliated to the labor movement or socialist parties, it succeeded in attracting more than a thousand students—mostly young—in each of its semesters and offered a broad range of courses that were taught by people of divergent intellectual and political orientations, including some free-market libertarians who were attracted to the school's nonsectarianism.

When I worked in a steel mill in the late 1950s, some of us formed a group that read current literature, labor history, and economics. I discussed books and magazine articles with some of my fellow workers in bars as well as on breaks. Tony Mazzocchi, who was at the same time a worker and an officer of a Long Island local of the Oil, Chemical & Atomic Workers Union, organized a similar group, and I knew of several other cases of young workers doing the same. Some of these groups evolved into rank-and-file caucuses that eventually contested the leadership of their local unions; others were mainly for the self-edification of the participants and had no particular political goals.

Beyond formal programs, ever since the industrializing era the working-class intellectual, although by no means visible in the United States, has been part of shop-floor culture. In almost every workplace there is a person or persons to whom other workers turn for information about the law, the union contract, or contemporary politics—or, equally important, as a source of general education. These individuals may or may not be schooled but, until the late 1950s, rarely had any college. Schools were not the primary source of their knowledge. They were, and are, largely self-educated. In my own case, having left Brooklyn College after less than a year, I worked in a variety of industrial production jobs. When I worked the midnight shift, I got off at 8:00 in the morning, ate breakfast, and spent four hours in the library before going home. Mostly I read American and European history and political economy, particularly the physiocrats, Adam Smith, David Ricardo, John Maynard Keynes, and Joseph Schumpeter. Marx's *Das Kapital* I read in high school and owned the three volumes.

My friend Russell Rommele, who worked in a nearby mill, was also an autodidact. His father was a first-generation German American brewery worker with no particular literary interests. But Russell had been exposed to a wide range of historical and philosophical works as a high school student at Saint Benedict's Prep, a Jesuit institution. The priests singled out Russell for the priesthood and mentored him in theology and social theory. The experience radicalized him, and he decided not to answer the call but to enter the industrial working class instead. Like me, he was active in the union and Newark Democratic Party politics. Working as an educator with a local union in the auto industry recently, I met several active unionists who are intellectuals. The major difference between them and those of my generation is that they are college graduates, although none claim to have acquired their love of learning or their analytic perspective from schools. One is a former member of a radical organization; another learned his politics from participation in a shop-based study group and union caucus organized by a member of a socialist group that dissolved in the mid-1990s when the group lost a crucial union election. In both instances, even after the demise of their organizational affiliations, they remain habituated to reading, writing, and union activity.

Parents, Neighborhood, and Class Culture

John Locke observes that, consistent with his rejection of innate ideas, even if conceptions of good and evil are present in divine or civil law, morality is constituted by reference to our parents, our relatives, and especially the "club" of peers to which we belong:

> He who imagines commendation and disgrace not to be strong motives to men to accommodate themselves to the opinions and rules of those with whom they converse seems little skilled in the nature or the history of mankind: the greatest part whereof we shall find govern themselves, chiefly, if not solely by this law of *fashion*; and so they do what keeps them in reputation with their company, little regard for the laws of God or the magistrate. (Locke 1954, bk. 1, ch. 28, no. 12, 478; emphasis in the original)

William James put the matter equally succinctly:

> A man's social self is the recognition which he gets from his mates. We are not only gregarious animals, liking to be in the sight of our fellows, but we have an innate propensity to get ourselves noticed, and noticed favorably, by our kind. No more fiendish punishment could be devised, were such a thing physically possible, than that

we should be turned loose in society and remain absolutely un-
noticed by all the members thereof. (James 1890, 351)

That the social worlds of peers and family are the chief referents
for the formation of the social self, neither philosopher had a
doubt. Each in his own fashion situates the individual in social
context, which provides a "common measure of virtue and vice"
(Locke 1954) even as they acknowledge that the ultimate choice
resides with the individual self. These and not the institutions,
even those that have the force of law, are the primary sources of
authority.

Hannah Arendt argues that education "by its very nature cannot forgo either authority or tradition." Nor can it base itself on
the presumption that children share an autonomous existence
from adults (Arendt 1961, 180–181). Yet schooling ignores the
reality of the society of kids at the cost of undermining its own
authority. The society of kids is in virtually all classes an alternative and opposition site of knowledge and of moral valuation.
We have already seen how working-class kids get working-class
jobs by means of their rebellion against school authority. Since
refusal and resistance are hallmarks of the moral order, the few
who will not obey the invocation to fail or to perform indifferently
in school often find themselves marginalized or expelled from the
community of kids. Although they adopt a rationality that can
be justified on eminently practical grounds, the long tradition
of rejection of academic culture has proven hard to break, even
in the wake of evidence that those working-class jobs to which
such students were oriented no longer exist. What is at stake in
adolescent resistance is the kids' perception that the blandishments of the adult world are vastly inferior to the pleasures of
their own. In the first place, the new service economy offers few
inducements: Wages are low, the jobs are boring, and the future
is bleak. And since the schools now openly present themselves
as a link in the general system of control, it may appear to some
students that cooperation is a form of self-deception.

If not invariably then in many households, parents provide to
the young a wealth of knowledge: the family mythologies that
feature an uncle or aunt, a grandparent, or an absent parent.
These stories are loosely based on actual events in which the
family member has distinguished her- or himself in various ways
that (usually) illustrate a moral virtue or defect so that the telling
constitutes a kind of didactic message. Even when the lessons

are not attached to an overt narrative, parable, or myth, we learn from our parents by their actions in relation to us and others. How do they deal with adversity? How do they address ordinary, everyday problems? What do they learn from their own trials and tribulations, and what do they say to us? What are our parents' attitudes toward money, joblessness, everyday life disruptions such as sudden acute illness or accidents? What do they learn from the endless conflicts with *their* parents over issues of sex, money, and household responsibilities?

The relative weight of parental as opposed to peer authority is an empirical question that cannot be decided in advance; what both have in common is their location within everyday life. The parents are likely to be more susceptible to the authority of law and its magistrates and, in a world of increasing uncertainty, will worry that if their children choose badly, they may be left behind. But the associations we make with our peers in everyday life provide the recognition that we crave, define what is worthy of praise or blame, and confer approbation or disapproval on our decisions. If an individual makes a choice that runs counter to that of his or her "company" or club, he or she must form or join a new "company" to confer the judgment of virtue on her or his action. This company must, of necessity, consist of "peers," the definition of which has proven fungible.

Religion, the law, and, among kids, school authorities face the obstacles erected by the powerful rewards and punishments meted out by the clubs with which people are affiliated. At a historical conjunction when the relentless pressure imposed by capital works to transform all labor into wage labor, thereby forcing every adult into the paid labor force, the society of kids increasingly occupies the space of civil society. The neighborhood, once dominated by women and small shopkeepers, has all but disappeared save for the presence of children and youth. As parents toil for endless hours to pay the ever-mounting debts incurred by home ownership, perpetual car and appliance payments, and the costs of health care, kids are increasingly on their own, and their relationships with each other have consequences for their conceptions of education and life.

Some recent studies and teacher observations have discovered a not inconsiderable reluctance among black students in elite universities to perform well in school, even those of professional and managerial family backgrounds. Many seem indifferent to arguments that show that school performance is a central prerequisite to better jobs and higher status in the larger work world. Among the more acute speculations is the conclusion that black students' resistance reflects an anti-intellectual bias and a hesitation, if not refusal, to enter the mainstream corporate world. Perhaps the charge of anti-intellectualism is better understood as healthy skepticism about the chance that a corporate career will provide the well-publicized satisfactions. There are similar indications among some relatively affluent white students. Although by no means a majority, some students are less enamored by the work world to which they, presumably, have been habituated by school, and especially by the prospect of perpetual work. In the third-tier universities, state and private alike, many students, apparently forced by their parents to enroll, wonder out loud why they are there. Skepticism about schooling still abounds even as they graduate high school and enroll in postsecondary schools in record numbers. According to one colleague of mine who teaches in a third-tier private university in the New York metropolitan area, many of these mostly suburban students "sleepwalk" through their classes, do not participate in class discussions, and are lucky to get C grades.

In the working-class neighborhoods—white, black, and Latino—the word is out: Given the absence of viable alternatives, you must try to obtain that degree, but this defines the limit of loyalty to the enterprise. Based on testimonies of high school and community college teachers, for every student who takes school knowledge seriously, there are twenty or more who are time-servers. Most are ill prepared to perform academic work, and since the community colleges and state four-year colleges and "teaching" universities simply lack the resources to provide the means by which such students' school performance can improve, there is little motivation for them beyond the credential to try to get an education.

In some instances, those who break from their club and enter the regime of school knowledge risk being drummed out of a lifetime of relationships with their peers. What has euphemistically been described as "peer pressure" bears, among other moral structures, on the degree to which kids are permitted to cross over the line into the precincts of adult authority. Although being a success in school is not equivalent to squealing on a friend or to the cops or transgressing some sacred moral code of the society of kids, it can come close to committing an act of betrayal. This is comprehensible only if the reader is willing to suspend the prejudice that schooling is tantamount to education and is an unqualified "good," as compared to the presumed evil of school failure or the decision of the slacker to rebel by refusing to succeed.

The concept of class, when invoked in either educational debates or any other politically charged discourse, generally refers to the white working class. Educational theory and practice treat blacks and Latinos, regardless of their economic positions, as unified, biological identities. That black kids from professional, managerial, and business backgrounds share more with their white counterparts than with working-class blacks is a fact generally ignored by most educational writers. Just as, in race discourse, "whites" are undifferentiated, since World War II, "race"—which refers in slightly different registers to people of African origin and those who migrated from Latin countries of Central and South America and the Caribbean—is treated as a unified category. The narrowing of the concept limits our ability to discern class at all. Although we must stipulate ethnic, gender, race, and occupational distinctions among differentiated strata of wage labor, with the exception of children of salaried professional and technical groups where the culture of schooling plays a decisive role, I want to suggest that class education transcends these distinctions. No doubt there are gradations among the strata that comprise this social formation. But the most privileged professional strata (physicians, attorneys, scientists, professors) and high-level managers are self-reproducing, not principally through schooling but through social networks. These include private schools, some of which are residential; clubs and associations; and, in suburban public schools, the self-selection of students on the basis of distinctions. Show me a school friendship between the son or daughter of a corporate manager and the child of a janitor or factory worker and I will show you a community service project to get the poorer student into one of the "select" colleges or universities such as Brown, Oberlin, or Wesleyan.

Schooling selects a fairly small number of children of the class of wage labor for genuine class mobility. In the first half of the twentieth century, having lost its appeal among middle-class youth, the Catholic Church turned to working-class students as a source of cadre recruitment. In my neighborhood of the East Bronx, two of my close childhood friends, both of Italian background, entered the priesthood. They were sons of construction workers, so the church provided their best chance to escape the hardships and economic uncertainties of manual labor. Another kid became a pharmacist because the local Catholic college, Fordham University, offered scholarships. A fourth was among the tiny coterie of students who passed the test for Bronx Science, one of the city's special schools, and became a science teacher. Almost everybody else remained a worker or, like my best friend, Kenny, went to prison.

Despite the well-publicized claim that anyone can escape their condition of social and economic birth—a claim reproduced by schools and by the media with numbing regularity—most working-class students, many of whom have some college credits but often do not graduate—end up in low- and middle-level service jobs that often do not pay a decent working-class wage. Owing to the steep decline of unionized industrial production jobs, those who enter factories increasingly draw wages that are substantially below union standards. Those who do graduate find work in computer jobs, although rarely at the professional levels. The relatively low-paid become K–12 teachers and health care professionals, mostly nurses and technicians, or enter the social services field as case workers, medical social workers, or line social welfare workers. The question I want to pose is whether these "professional" occupations represent genuine mobility.

During the postwar economic boom, which made possible a significant expansion of spending for schools, the social services, and administration of public goods, the public sector workplace became a favored site of black and Latino recruitment, mainly for clerical, maintenance, and entry-level patient care jobs in hospitals and other health care facilities. Within several decades, a good number advanced to middle-level jobs such as registered nursing, but not in all sections of the country. As unionization spread to the nonprofit private sector as well as to public employment in the 1960s and 1970s, these jobs paid enough to enable many to enjoy what became known as a "middle-class" living standard as well as a measure of job security offered by union security and civil service status. Although it is true that such "security" has often been observed in its breach, the traditional deal made by teachers, nurses, and social workers was to trade higher incomes for job security. But after about 1960, spurred by the resurgent civil rights movement, these "second-level" professionals—white and black—began to see themselves as workers more than professionals: They formed unions, struck for higher pay and shorter hours, and assumed a very unprofessional adversarial stance toward institutional authority. Contracts stipulated higher salaries;

definite hours—a sharp departure from professional ideology —seniority as a basis for layoffs, just like any industrial contract; and substantial vacation and sick leave.

Their assertion of working-class values and social position may have been strategic; indeed, it inspired the largest wave of union organizing since the 1930s. But, together with the entrance of huge numbers of women and blacks into the public and quasi–public sector workforces, it was also a symptom of the proletarianization of the second-tier professions. Several decades later, salaried physicians made a similar discovery; they formed unions and struck against high malpractice insurance costs as much as the onerous conditions imposed on their autonomy by health maintenance organizations and government authorities bent on cost containment, often at the physicians' expense. More to the point, the steep rise of public employees' salaries and benefits posed the question of how to maintain services in times of fiscal austerity, which might be due to an economic downturn or to probusiness tax policies. The answer has been that the political and public officials told employees that the temporary respite from the classical trade union trade-off was over. All public employees have suffered relative deterioration in their salaries and benefits. Since the mid-1970s fiscal crises, beginning in New York City, they have experienced layoffs for the first time since the Depression. And their unions have been in a continuous concessionary bargaining mode for decades. In the politically and ideologically repressive environment of the past twenty-five years, the class divide has sharpened. Ironically, in the wake of the attacks by legislatures and business against their hard-won gains, in the early 1980s the teachers' unions abandoned their militant class posture and reverted to professionalism and to a center-right political strategy.

In truth, schools are learning sites, even if only for a handful of intellectual knowledge. In the main, they transmit the instrumental logic of credentialism, together with their transformation from institutions of discipline to those of control, especially in working-class districts. Even talented, dedicated teachers have more difficulty reaching kids and convincing them that the life of the mind may hold unexpected rewards, even if the career implications of critical thought are not apparent. The breakdown of the mission of public schools has produced varied forms of disaffection; if school violence has abated in some places, it does not signify the decline of gangs and other clubs that signify the autonomous world of youth. The society of kids is more autonomous because, in contrast to the 1960s, today's authorities no longer offer hope. Instead, under the doctrine of control they threaten punishment, which includes, although it is not necessarily associated with, incarceration. However, the large number of drug busts of young black and Latino men should not be minimized. With over a million blacks, more than 3 percent of the African American population—most of them young—is within the purview of the criminal justice system; thus, the law may be viewed as a more or less concerted effort to counter by force of the power of peers. This may be regarded in the context of the failure of schools. Of course, more than 300 years ago, John Locke knew the limits of the ability of the magistrates—indeed, of any adult authority—to overcome the power of the society of kids (Giroux 2000).

Conclusion

What are the requisite changes that would transform schools from credential mills and institutions of control to a site of education that prepares young people to see themselves as active participants in the world? As my analysis implies, the fundamental condition is to abolish the high-stakes standardized tests that dominate the curriculum, subordinate teachers to the role of drill masters, and subject students to stringent controls. I do not mean to eliminate the need for evaluative tools. The essay is a fine measure of both writing ability and the student's grasp of literature, social science, and history. Although I must admit that math and science as much as language proficiency require considerable rote learning, the current curriculum and pedagogy in these fields include neither a historical account of the changes in scientific and mathematical theory nor a metaconceptual explanation of what the disciplines are about. Nor are courses in language at the secondary level ever concerned with etymological issues, comparative cultural study of semantic differences, or other topics that might relieve the boredom of rote learning by providing depth of understanding. The broader understanding of science in the modern world—its relation to technology, war, and medicine, for example—should surely be integrated into the curriculum; some of these issues appear in the textbooks, but teachers rarely discuss them because they are busy preparing students for the high-stakes tests in which knowledge of the social contexts for science, language, and math are not included.

I agree with Arendt that education "cannot forgo either authority or tradition." But authority must be earned rather than assumed, and the transmission of tradition needs to be critical rather than worshipful. If teachers were allowed to acknowledge student skepticism and incorporate kids' knowledge into the curriculum by making what they know—especially popular music and television—the object of rigorous study, they might be treated with greater respect. But there is no point denying the canon; one of the more egregious conditions of subordination is the failure of schools to expose students to their best exemplars, for people who have no cultural capital are condemned to social and political marginality, let alone deprived of some of the pleasures to be derived from encounters with genuine works of art. The New York City Board of Education (now the Department of Education) mandates that during every semester high school English classes read a Shakespeare play and one or two works of nineteenth-century English literature. However, it affords little or no access to the best Russian novels of the nineteenth century; no opportunities to examine some of the most influential works of Western philosophy, beginning and carrying on from the Milesians through Plato, Aristotle, and the major figures of "modern philosophy"; and no social and historical context for what is learned—thus, tradition is observed more in the breach than in its practice. And when, under budgetary pressures, elementary and secondary schools cut music and art from the curriculum, they deprive students of the best sources for cultivating the creative imagination. Schools fulfill their responsibility to students and their communities when, at every level, they offer a program of systematic, critical learning that simultaneously provides students with access to the rich traditions of so-called Western thought, history, and the arts, including literature, and opens parallel vistas of Africa, Asia, and Latin America (Aronowitz 2000, ch. 7).

Finally, the schools should relieve themselves of their ties to corporate interests and reconstruct the curriculum along lines of genuine intellectual endeavor. Nor should the schools be seen as career conduits, although this function will be difficult to displace—among other reasons because in an era of high economic anxiety, many kids and their parents worry about the future and seek some practical purchase on it. It will take some doing to convince them that their best leg up is an education. It is unlikely in the present environment but possible in some places.

I could elaborate these options; this chapter is only an outline. In order to come close to their fulfillment, at least three things are needed. First, we require a conversation concerning the nature and scope of education and the limits of schooling as an educational site. Along with this, theorists and researchers need to link their knowledge of popular culture, and culture in the anthropological sense—that is, everyday life—with the politics of education. Specifically, we need to examine why in late capitalist societies, the public sphere withers while the corporatization process penetrates every sphere of life.

Second, we need teachers who, by their own education, are intellectuals who respect children and want to help them obtain a genuine education, regardless of their social class. For this we need a new regimen of teacher education founded on the idea that the educator must be well educated. It would surely entail abolishing the current curricula of most education schools, if not the schools themselves. The endless courses on "teaching methods" would be replaced with courses in the natural and social sciences, mathematics, philosophy, history, and literature. Some of these courses would address the relation of education, in all its forms, to these subjects' social and historical context. In effect, the teacher would become an intellectual, capable of the critical appropriation of world histories and cultures.

Third, we need a movement of parents, students, teachers, and the labor movement armed with a political program directed toward forcing legislatures to adequately fund schooling at the federal, state, and local levels and boards of education to deauthorize the high-stakes standardized tests that currently drive the curriculum and pedagogy (Aronowitz and Giroux 1985).

Having proposed these changes, we need to remain mindful of the limitations of schooling and the likelihood that youth will acquire knowledge outside schools that prepares them for life, such as sex, the arts, where to find jobs, how to bind with other people, how to fight, how to love and hate. The deinstitutionalization of education does not require abandoning schools. But they should be rendered benign, removed as much as possible from the tightening grip of the corporate warfare state. In turn, teachers must resist becoming agents of the prison system, of the drug companies, of corporate capital. In the last instance, the best chance for education resides in the communities, in social movements, and in the kids themselves.

◇

3

The World Turned Upside Down—Again

In *The World Turned Upside Down,* the great British historian Christopher Hill addresses the transformation that took place in the seventeenth century in England. This was a century of revolution—two revolutions, to be exact, in 1640 and 1688, which never really succeeded in completely overturning established power but did destroy the prevailing forms of social and economic authority and utterly changed everyday life in the countryside and city alike. Although the previous century had witnessed the rise of mercantile capitalism, the countryside was still dominated by feudal relations. The seventeenth century was the time when England embarked on its modern age, in which social relations became almost thoroughly capitalist. During the seventeenth, eighteenth, and early nineteenth centuries, many of the cities of England were populated by people who had come from the countryside because of the enclosures.

The enclosures in England meant the end of the old system of land tenure and the rise of the new system of individual capitalist farming as well as corporate farming, which was far more advanced in England than it was in North America. Its consequence was that it produced the English working class and the modern phenomenon of unemployment and underemployment. Poverty was the mode of existence for large numbers of people in England during that period. It was clear to contemporaries of the eighteenth and as late as the nineteenth century—poets such as Percy Bysshe Shelley and Thomas Hood were prominent among them—that industrial capitalism was a system of injustice. It was clear to them that unless there was some rebellion by those who had been disenfranchised by the whirlwind changes that had taken place in England, what had been understood as a version of the British Enlightenment—the Enlightenment as represented by people such as John Locke—would become essentially a hollow phrase.

I don't think it comes as a surprise to anyone that we are now in a century (and maybe it started thirty-five years ago, some people say around 1973) in which our world has been turned upside down. We are in a period—and we're only at the beginning—of enormous dislocation, of the kinds of transformations that have been described as disenfranchisement, in which literally hundreds of millions of people have seen their lives change. Let me start with the most dramatic examples. In China, estimates range from 150 to 200 million peasants who have been literally driven off the land. In China, and to a large extent in India, Latin America, and Africa, we are entering a new era of enclosures that makes the English enclosures that have been celebrated in books and studies look like a prelude, a very small event. The English intelligentsia was extremely exercised about events that affected 300,000 or 400,000, perhaps half a million, people, but we now see hundreds of millions of people driven off the land into the great cities of Asia as well as enormous migrations to the United States, Canada, and western Europe. The old story that capital can move but labor is relatively stationary is no longer the case. Labor can move—whether it wants to or not. And as people come into the cities—Shanghai, New York, Los Angeles, Toronto, and other places around the world—they find themselves in many cases at sea. Not only is there unemployment, but they find themselves part of an economy that is no longer able to accommodate that immigration.

That's one element of the world turned upside down. The second element is one that many people have the greatest problem coming to terms with: The period of postwar expansion that began in 1945 and pretty much began to end in the 1970s—the thirty years of expansion—is definitively over. And all the optimism that comes from neoliberal economics, from politicians and businesspeople, wittingly or unwittingly, is nothing short of a sham. These economies in which we live are restructured economies, the labor market in particular, and they are largely stagnant. There is a growth in certain parts of the world economy, but it is in large part engendered by capital that comes out of the metropoles of western Europe and the United States, which are engendering growth in India, China, and so on. We have trouble with this recognition because we are now in a period in which not only manual labor but also intellectual labor—the main agent of enfranchisement—is being disenfranchised. The idea that a PhD and master's degree qualified one for a relatively secure position was a watchword until about the 1980s. I am a faculty member of the largest urban university in North America; it has 225,000 students and is growing. It has roughly 14,000 faculty members, 8,500 of whom work on a part-time, contingent, temporary basis, teaching 6, 9, or 15 hours a week on different campuses around the New York area—what we used to call in Los Angeles "freeway flyers." We are in a period when the good job is rapidly becoming the preserve of a tiny minority.

Although academic labor, along with the labor of large portions of the working poor, is suffering this transformation in extremis, the changes are spreading to other categories as well. Microsoft, the largest software manufacturer in the world, has a two-tier system for its computer analysts and engineers. Workers on the first tier get a relatively modest salary but also get stock options and benefits such as health insurance and paid vacations; workers on the second tier are contract laborers who have become the majority of employees at Microsoft. The company's profits are covered up by its efforts in medical and educational charity. The business is in billions and the charity in tens of millions. What Microsoft is trying to do, in terms of both its labor practices and competitive practices, is to use its generous support of such issues as innovation in high schools to create an image of generosity. In this respect, the corporation is emulating its great predecessors, such as the Carnegie Corporation, the Ford Corporation, and the Robert Wood Johnson Corporation, all of which engaged in nefarious practices and created foundations that, however autonomous, yet carry the name of the company. And that's the name of the game in the United States. We have this emphasis, especially in education, on corporate generosity, and at the same time the world is being turned upside down in everyday life by global corporate capital.

Everyday life in the United States has changed dramatically. Lifelong learning, which I'll come to later in this chapter, is no longer a desired goal but an absolute necessity, at least for those people who had become accustomed for those two or three generations to having a job they could count on, not just in a mill, a factory, or an assembly line but in retail, wholesale, or small-scale manufacturing. Those jobs are no longer secure. In my short and happy life, I've had four careers. My first one was as an industrial worker, after a brief stint as a college student. I was one of those people who could never sit in a classroom unless I was teaching it. I was an industrial worker and union organizer for fifteen years, and those were two different jobs—one was working on the shop floor in the steel industry, and the other was actually organizing in the field. Then, for various reasons, I left full-time union work, partly because I stopped believing that unions were transformative forces in our society. That may or may not be true, but I thought so at the time, and I became an administrator in the City of New York Manpower and Career Development Agency, part of the anti-poverty program, and established the first public service careers program in New York City. Subsequently I became an organizer again, but a community organizer this time, and then a director of the first experimental public high school in New York since the Depression. The aim of that high school was to try to link work with education, and that's what I'm going to talk about primarily. And then of course, for my fourth career, I was a community college teacher on Staten Island from 1972 to 1976. I taught the usual nine courses a year, and I did this for four years. I was lucky that I had a lot of energy because in the middle of this I wrote a book called *False Promises* (Aronowitz 1973), which has sold a lot of copies and got me a full professorship at the University of California–Irvine three years after its publication.

The point I'm making is that my occupational trajectory, which was considered quite unusual in the 1960s and 1970s until I became a full professor without having gone through the ritual torture of the tenure process, is no longer an anomaly but is becoming more usual in that we will live our lives doing four or even five things—and I'm referring not only to manual or technical workers but also to professional and scientific people. In the United States, for example, it is as difficult for scientific workers to get an academic job that gives them opportunities for research as it is to get an academic job in the humanities and social sciences, and maybe a little worse. People in their forties are still working as postdocs—biologists, physicists, and chemists—because they do not want to work in private industry, but there's no space for them in a university setting to do the kind of work for which they thought they were being trained. So we're in a scary period because lifelong learning—learning new occupations, learning new workplaces, learning new regions, having a different sense of space—is becoming more and more common. In the United States, 29 percent of new university hires since 2000 are tenure-track in teaching. The consequence of this, of course, is that 71 percent are not tenure-track—they're in two-year, three-year, one-year, one-semester, part-time, contingent jobs. In many of those cases, they've gotten a PhD without the possibility of a full-time job in the discipline in which they were trained. As a result, many are leaving academia, leaving the work they loved and thought they would be doing for the rest of their lives.

The consequences affect not only individuals but the country, the people as such, for three elements of education are no longer being addressed in our institutions. The first element is the possibility of self-knowledge, the understanding of the relation between the self and the world, how we as people connect with the environment in which we live. The second is the recognition that we know of only one science, the science of history, that teaches us to know where we've come from. We can't know who we are unless we know where we've been. Our ancestors are unknown to us—we don't know their languages; we don't know what they did or where they came from. We may know something about why they came here, but once they arrived in North America, everything preceding that moment is forgotten, and our education system has done everything it can to help us forget who we are. And I don't mean only racially, ethnically, and in terms of gender but also who we are in terms of the history of humankind. Historical memory has almost been lost.

But the third fundamental element of education is perhaps the most important—if we really think, as many do, that education is connected to the growth, the resilience, and the vitality of a whole society, then we must be a society in which those who inhabit the planet have the space and the time to create the new. As we know, the creation of the new proceeds from the critique of what is as well as what was. We cannot create the new in a vacuum; we create the new by saying that the previous paradigm can no longer explain key aspects of our physical and social worlds. The year 2005 was the one hundredth anniversary of Einstein's publication of his special theory of relativity. He argued that the Newtonian paradigm was important, but he wanted to suggest a new paradigm. In simple terms, he found that there is no absolute space or absolute time, that the relationship between space and time depends on the context in which we do the thinking and the work of defining it. Controversially, Heisenberg concluded, if that's the case, then we have an element of indeterminacy in our understanding of the physical world because we ourselves are part of the physical world: The act of knowing is not one of distance but one of intimate relation.

Those were creative acts. Where are we going to find the creativity if we throw our intellectual labor into the garbage can? Where are we going to find the people who can actually invent the new, who can address the world turned upside down in a way that does not repeat the seventeenth-, eighteenth-, and nineteenth-century histories of blasphemy, of degradation, of class privilege? We can find them only in the people who have the time and space for reflection. Our job as intellectuals is to reflect on our situation and on the situation of people around us and to be able, on the basis of that reflection, to come up with new ideas. Ideas, even though they are conditioned by the circumstances in which they are produced, have an autonomy that is irreplaceable by training. Ideas have an autonomy that is irreplaceable by education about the past, education about technique, education about method. Ideas are leaps of radical imagination—and radical imagination proceeds from radical critique, if only implicitly.

One of the characteristics of our period is that the concept not only of the intellectual himself or herself but of the political and public intellectual is being relegated to the sidelines, to the margins, unless those intellectuals are prepared to reproduce the past as if it was eternal. We know that every hegemonic, every ruling system wants to make its system natural—when a prominent journalist such as Thomas Friedman can say it's too late, that neoliberalism will continue and that free-market economies are the only way that we can reproduce any set of given ends, what he is doing is reproducing hegemonic ideologies (Friedman 2005). And he's getting people to repeat what he says like parrots. Our job is to say no, not so fast, never mind whether or not you have any degree of an alternative—the first thing to recognize is that, around the world, in the antiglobalization movement, in the social forums that are developing in 200 countries, people are saying we have to create a civil society in which the concept of the creativity of intellectual ideas and the possibility of social justice have to be put on the front burner. And these people have slowed down the forward march of the World Bank and the International Monetary Fund and the World Trade Organization through resistance and protest. But the problem obviously is to find alternatives. And that can't be done unless you have an educational system that says alternatives are what we want. So the question of lifelong learning is not whether the individual can learn to adapt to changing circumstances, not whether adaptation, which is an old biological law, is possible. We can stipulate that adaptation is possible—there'll be a few hundred million people who will die in the process of AIDS, of diphtheria, of dysentery and a whole variety of other things, but there will be a society of some kind left. The question is whether people will actually be able to intervene, if they'll be able to become global as well as national citizens in the sense that they can say, no, this is what we want, and that is what we don't want. Making that happen is much more difficult than mobilizing resistance. It requires in the first case that large numbers of people—and I don't argue that everyone is going to be able to do this; I'm not naive—know the difference between description and concept.

Many of us know how to describe; few of us know how to conceptualize a situation, to give it a sense of coherence and then be able to address it in relation to the alternatives. So when I speak today of lifelong learning and its relationship to work, I'm asking whether the work of who we are is to foster the possibility of educational systems that can help people develop a sense of themselves in relation to the larger world: a sense of history, a sense of structure, and a sense of how they themselves can begin to re-create the world. You may think this idea is utopian, and guess what—it is. But so is the special theory of relativity; so is the Copernican revolution in relation to the Ptolemaic revolution of the Aristotelian period. So was the Communist Manifesto. So is almost any new idea that has come before us. Now, the problem we face is what to do practically, especially those of us who are labor or union oriented. I'm on the negotiating committee of my own union, and I suggest that one of the things that is missing is that we don't have debate. In England we don't have debate; in the United States we don't have debate; I don't know how often we have debate in Canada. We have to foster debate about globalization, what to do about industrialization, what the alternatives are to simply accepting things as if they were natural.

The Argentine workers discovered that shuttering industrial plants was not a natural phenomenon. They went back into the factories to operate them themselves on a cooperative, nonprofit basis. What other alternatives might we have? There are moves in a similar direction in Canada and the United Kingdom. We ought to think about changes in the nature of unions so they don't remain only shop-floor based but are based in the larger community needs of members, of workers, of ordinary people. How do we deal with the housing crisis? How do we deal with high rents, high costs of schooling? How do we create institutions of higher education and elementary and secondary educational schools that actually fulfill educational and not training objectives? These are the kinds of questions we should be asking and answering. I recently saw a report on Ontario learning and labor. The report was very pretty, extremely visually interesting, which I think corresponds to the situation we're in, but it had no new ideas. It talked about adaptation; it argued that we should convince business to undertake training, that we should have more counseling to educate people about the changing nature of the workplace, the changing nature of the economy. Instead of adaptation we ought to have debates about the changing nature of the economy—we should not accept any of these things as natural facts. We should recognize that these changes have been socially and historically constituted, and we should be developing programs that help people ask the questions rather than giving the fast answers—and ask the questions largely about alternatives.

We are all so busy doing things that we never have time for thinking. I am not one to quote Martin Heidegger very often, for a variety of reasons, not the least of which is that I'm Jewish, but he does have a very important message when he asks the question, Are we thinking? (Heidegger 1968). And he goes through a whole series of exercises, literally thought experiments, to determine whether we are thinking yet. I want to suggest that we are not yet thinking.

PART II

HIGHER EDUCATION OR HIGHER TRAINING?

◇

4

Higher Education as a Public Good

I

For the first time since the late 1960s, when student demonstrations and occupations forced open admissions in many public colleges and universities, higher education has become a major public issue. There are three questions that define the debate. First, legislative and executive authorities must be committed to maintaining public higher education at an adequate level of funding for institutions to offer a high-quality education to students. Second is the so-called access debate: who should be admitted and who should be excluded from higher education. Put another way, should higher education be a "right," like elementary and secondary schooling? Or should it be, as for our European counterparts, a privilege reserved for those with a requisite level of academic achievement? In this conversation we hear comments like "After all, not everyone should be in college; what about the millions who work in factories or offices?" Finally, especially in recent years, the question of curriculum has been thrust closer to center stage. The chief bone of contention is whether the once presumed liberal arts should be available to every college student—indeed, should every student regardless of discipline be required to imbibe at least a sampling of literature, philosophy, history, and the social sciences? Some have argued—and many institutions have agreed—that students in technical and professional areas such as computer science, engineering, and even natural science should, in the service of proficiency, largely be exempted from such encumbrances. Of course this argument applies both to high-level technical universities such as Carnegie Mellon University, Rensselaer Polytechnic Institute, and Case Western Reserve University and to the large number of community colleges whose "mission" is now almost exclusively confined to preparing trained workers for the corporations with whom they have developed close relationships.

Higher education has become prominent on the political screen as the widespread perception that earning a bachelor's degree is the absolute precondition for obtaining a better niche in the occupational structure. But as postsecondary credentials have become a necessary qualification for nearly every technical let alone professional job, higher-education costs—both tuition and living expenses—have skyrocketed and, egregiously, routinely exceed inflation rates. At the same time, more than ever students and their families are seeking places in private colleges and universities and, with the exception of a handful of elite public research universities, interpret failure to secure admission to leading private schools as a major personal and economic defeat. For the bare truth is that in the last decade of neoliberal economic and social ideologies, public postsecondary schools are taking a severe beating in the commonwealth. In the current environment, budget cuts and downsizing are prescribed by policy-makers as the zeitgeist has shifted to the view that only the marketplace represents quality and anything connected to public goods that does not submit itself to the business environment is a second-rate article.

The effect of this persistent and merciless attack on public higher education has been to demoralize faculty and prompt conservative-dominated legislatures to impose a regimen of permanent austerity that, with the exception of a handful of public research universities—notably those of the University of California (UC) and of the Big Ten—has resulted in sharpening the distinction between the two research tiers of the academic system on the one hand and the third tier of public teaching institutions, both senior and community colleges, on the other. Former Berkeley Chancellor Clark Kerr's notorious proposal, first announced in 1958 and inscribed in the California state systems in the early 1960s, that the research tiers be fiercely defended from the horde by establishing a clear separation between those institutions that produce knowledge and those that transmit it has succeeded beyond his and his critics' wildest expectations. Today this mantra has been enhanced by the proposition that only certain teaching institutions, some private four-year colleges, are "excellent" enough to qualify for the transmission task.

The Kerr plan was no mere speculation; it contained a detailed program to ensure the separation. Research university faculty were to teach one or two courses a semester, and could even purchase their teaching time with research grants. In contrast, the third-tier universities and colleges obliged faculty to teach three or four courses, and community colleges typically required five a semester. The reward systems would be different insofar as publication would play a distinctly subordinate role in the third tier. At the same time, Kerr envisioned substantial salary differentials. The only means for moving upward in the new academic system would be through research and writing—and, of course, administration.

Yet the tiering of higher education hit a snag in the 1960s. Two distinct movements for university reform gained momentum. The first was the insistent demands by black, Latino, and working-class students for access to the institutions as a sign of equality as well as equality of opportunity; the second was the profound dissatisfaction by mostly white, middle-class students in elite universities with the growing trend toward focusing on technical and scientific knowledge production in what Kerr called the "multiversity." At Berkeley and elsewhere in the early 1960s they came together in a mass student movement in which these two quite different thrusts were merged in the struggle against the emergence of the corporate university. The success of the demand for extending higher-education access to virtually any high school graduate depended, in part, on the authority of the civil rights movement, which undergirded student protest, and on the crisis of legitimacy of the national government in the wake of its unpopular Vietnam War policies. It was made feasible as well by the relative buoyancy of the war-suffused U.S. economy, which enabled federal and state governments to supply the funds needed to expand the public university system.

Students protested on questions of curriculum and for a time forced faculty and university administrators to give some ground. Although the Berkeley Free Speech Movement was detonated by the technocratic Kerr administration's policy barring "outside" political groups from the campus, its apogee was in the achievement of significant curricular reforms. In the UC system, Berkeley, San Diego, and Irvine students wanted the right to select their own courses and choose instructors to teach them. In some

places they demanded and won exemption from course requirements, especially from large introductory classes, and protested
the authoritarian pedagogical styles of some professors, which
prompted the most obdurate among the faculty to resign and go
elsewhere. These struggles, which dominated many campuses
until the emergence of the antiwar movement in the late 1960s,
succeeded in changing higher education's culture for the next
twenty years, even though the student movement shifted its emphasis from university reform to war protest—a decision that has
had profound consequences. Beginning with Harvard's reimposi-
tion of the core curriculum in 1979 and the ebbing of the student
movement, faculty and administration slowly regained the upper
hand over the next two decades.

With the triumph of market principles in higher education,
meaning everything from student enrollments to curriculum
and tuition costs was determined by the sales effort, the job
market, and the ebbing of the black freedom movement and
mass antiwar movement, the astounding expansion of public
colleges and universities came to screeching halt. Suddenly in
this most advanced of advanced industrial societies, corporate
and government economists announced a "fiscal crisis" in public
goods, including higher education. The "public" (read business,
professional, and corporate farm interests) was simply unwilling
to pay the bill for education, health, and other elements of the
social wage, especially for those who, as the media mantra never
ceased to remind us, were largely the "undeserving" poor. They
suggested that the way out of the crisis was to impose user taxes
on public goods; students and their families should be required
to substantially pay for public higher education. If enrollees in
private schools were willing to pay large tuition fees, why not those
in public universities?

Conservatives in and out of higher education never accepted
open admissions. By their lights, the democratization of access
to public colleges, and to the elite and private schools as well, degraded the value of the degree. For on the heels of the sea change
in public higher education brought about by the entrance into
colleges and universities in the late 1960s of perhaps a million
additional blacks, Latinos, and other racialized minorities (who,
absent the civil rights movement, would never have reached these
institutions' gates), there was considerable pressure on the Ivy
League and other private schools to undertake policies that, in effect, modified their traditions of cronyism and nepotism and their

meritocratic bias. Contrary to popular myth, neither the public nor the private sector was indiscriminate in their admissions policies; open admissions never meant that students with low grade-point averages and lower scores on SAT and other standardized tests gained entrance to public senior colleges, let alone the private elite colleges and universities. Although these schools often provide remediation services to students, especially those who failed the math sections of the SAT or did not take enough math to qualify for university-level courses, admission policies remain selective. In most states, open admissions has been confined to community colleges and some third-tier senior colleges.

Abetted by the media, which seem to swallow almost any attack on public higher education emanating from conservative education think tanks such as the Hudson and Manhattan Institutes, the educational Right has mounted what may be the most concerted and coordinated attack against public goods in this century. With the possible exception of the widespread belief that charter schools and vouchers are needed to radically issue a wake-up call to public elementary and secondary education, in recent educational history educational policy is more than ever driven by the conservative ideology of hierarchy and privatization.

II

The rise of mass public higher education in America was a result of several influences, chiefly those that resulted from the problems associated with the post–World War II era. Perhaps the most important piece of social engineering after the war was the Servicemen's Readjustment Act of 1944, popularly known as the GI Bill of Rights. At the urging of President Franklin D. Roosevelt, who feared mass unemployment in the postwar period, Congress passed a bill providing returning veterans with income support for a one-year period and funds to enter educational programs, including higher education. Between 1945 and 1952, a million veterans entered mostly private colleges and universities armed with the price of tuition and modest living expenses. All manner of institutions, including the Ivies and other elite schools, gladly accepted these veterans and the government money that accompanied them.

Actually, public higher education has a long history. Founded in 1847 by Townsend Harris, the Free Academy of New York was intended to provide an opportunity for "talented" young people of modest means to gain the benefits of a college education on a tuition-free basis. The municipal college movement spread slowly and never really embraced a large number of communities, but its example inspired parallel efforts at the state level. After the founding of City College, the successor to the Free Academy, the most substantial event in the emergence of public higher education was the Morrell Act of 1862. Under the sign of economic growth, the federal government supplied large tracts of federal land to states willing to found universities for the purpose of providing general education in all areas of learning, but chiefly scientific and technical research and assistance to agriculture and industry. Thus, it is no accident that many of our leading research universities were established as land-grant colleges at a time when private colleges and universities were little more than finishing schools for the economic and political elites and training institutes for the clergy, lawyers, and business administrators.

Within a half century many Midwestern states, several in the Northeast, and several in the South established so-called land-grant colleges. Despite the intention of the Morrell Act, many of these institutions remained glorified teachers' colleges, but some, such as the Universities of Michigan, Wisconsin, Illinois, and Indiana, took on characteristics identified with the modern research university. Together with the University of California–Berkeley and Cornell University, along with Harvard, the Massachusetts Institute of Technology, and Princeton among the private schools, they constituted the basis for the development of the modern research university, which came into its own with the government's rearmament program on the eve of World War II.

After World War II, the state universities and public municipal colleges also benefited from the largesse of the federal government. In fact, under the imperatives of the Korean War, which drafted more than 1 million men and women, funding for the GI Bill was extended—an illustration of the irony that, until recently, war has been good for social welfare of all kinds. And the Cold War provided a substantial boost to the research programs of public state universities. Having exploded a nuclear device by 1949, the Soviet Union accelerated its military nuclear and space programs, which among other windfalls prompted the U.S. government to support higher education in a concerted attempt to stem the "Sputnik" effect (especially after the Soviets beat the U.S. space program by sending a manned device into space): the alleged

Soviet superiority in space exploration and its perceived nuclear parity. By the late 1950s the federal government had committed itself to long-term support for postsecondary schooling, especially to students seeking careers in natural science and technology, but also supported the humanities and social sciences through, among other programs, the Defense Education Act. And states were pouring substantial funds into higher education as well. By 1960 the public sector was larger than the private sector and a decade later accounted for more than 70 percent of student enrollment.

After more than sixty years, when public colleges and universities gradually supplanted private schools as the dominant sector of higher education, we are now witnessing the return of tradition. In the shadow of neoliberal ideology, according to which private is better, the private sector of postsecondary education is growing faster than the public and, perhaps more to the point, is widely perceived as superior. If the measure of quality is, for all practical purposes, equivalent to a school's ability to exclude students because of the institution's marketability, then the elite private schools have gained substantially on similarly placed public institutions. To be sure, some public systems such as the Big Ten and the UC schools are still highly competitive in the ranking frenzy that has overwhelmed parents and educators, but private institutions such as Brown, Harvard, and Yale reject more than four of every five applicants, and many others such as the "little" Ivies have similar records of exclusion.

The economic reasons for this state of affairs are not difficult to discern: Faced with deregulation and the threat of globalization, Congress and state legislatures hurried to court the favor of business interests. They deprogressivized taxes, made it difficult to raise public funds for public education by raising the standard by which such bills would be passed, and moved authority for new taxes to the voters. In California, Massachusetts, and many other states, the referendum, whose origin was in the progressive era's skeptical response to the "bought" politicians of those years, was used to provoke what Richard Elman has called "the Poorhouse State (Elman 1966). In California, the Northeast, and the Southwest, for example, annual budget cuts, either in monetary or real terms, have been imposed by many state legislatures. (By "real terms," I refer to a stagnant or slightly increased budget that fails to match inflation rates.) The consequent systematic replacement of full-time professors with adjuncts, teaching assistants, and temporary professors in teaching undergraduate curricula is rife. The slide in salaries for full-timers (where increases lag behind the cost of living) has inclined those with some lateral mobility to move to private institutions. We have also witnessed the drying up of funds for construction and maintenance of aging physical plants, except when a governor finds an opportunity to reward a generous donor to his or her campaign.

But money tells only part of the story. The private colleges and universities have mounted a huge public relations effort to persuade parents and prospective students with resources to pay that the advantages they offer are worth the price of exorbitant tuition, especially in comparison to the costs of public education. They brazenly attempt to capture disaffected students from public education and shed no tears when their appeal results in huge debt for families that can ill afford the price of private tuition. Needless to say, getting a good education is only part of the consideration. Above all, the private institutions, especially the elite schools, offer prestige (and social capital), which may lead to effective job placement in the corporate world, valuable contacts among peers for future jobs, and a more comfortable student life, exemplified by better facilities such as dorms, sport facilities, and recreation centers.

Beyond these trumpeted advantages is the systematic attack against public higher education emanating from right-wing think tanks and conservatives whose views find a receptive ear in the media. For example, the New York media gave enormous and favorable publicity to a recent report on City University of New York (CUNY) by a mayoral commission headed by former Yale president Benno Schmidt, among whose members were conservatives of all stripes and employees of the mayor. The commission found the 200,000-student CUNY to be "adrift" and in need of reform. It recommended major changes, among them further administrative centralization to assure that the reform program would be effective; erosion of faculty governance because the faculty was judged to be a leading obstacle to changes anticipated by the report; provisions to undermine the university's professional autonomy; "mission differentiation," a code term for creating several new tiers in the system to assure that the top tier is protected against the community colleges; and a hard look at tenure with a view to abolishing or severely restricting it. Schmidt is currently the leader of the Edison Project, a for-profit corporation that organizes and consults with public schools in search of privatization around the country. The commission also included Heather McDonald, a fellow of the Manhattan Institute, a conservative think tank, and an array of similarly oriented members. Shortly after issuing the report, which became a blueprint for the new university administration that took office at the end of 1999, Schmidt became vice chair of CUNY's board of trustees.

The prospective transformation of CUNY from a beacon of open admissions for the city's minority and working-class population to a genuine competitor in the elite game that has swept through higher education would be a step back into the pre-1960s era, when New York City's four colleges were held to a higher standard than nearly all the area's other higher-education institutions. To gain entrance to these tuition-free schools, students were required to earn grade-point averages of 85 or higher from a secondary school system that was second to none in the entire country. In fact, the four original city colleges and Baruch, the system's business college, still require high GPAs as well as passing grades on each of three "placement" (that is, admission) tests. The difference in the intervening forty years is that the majority admitted based on passing grades are blacks, Latinos, and Asians; for this reason, the grades are considered by CUNY's detractors to be "inflated."

Curiously, the charge of grade inflation, when made at and tacitly acknowledged by several Ivy League schools, has failed to diminish those universities' prestige. Having recently abolished its A-plus grade, Princeton is an example of a school that, because it rejects many more applicants than it accepts and has a sumptuous endowment, retains its elite standing. Similarly, in an article on the alleged revival of Columbia University, *New York Times* reporter Karen Arenson pointed out that one of the major indicators that the school enjoys a revived reputation is that it admitted only 13.7 percent of applicants in 2004, a figure that placed it second only to Brown, whose rejection rate is 87 percent. In none of the recent reports on the booming private college industry has the question of educational quality figured in the evaluation of the universities' success. The measure of quality seems to rely heavily on whether school admission is considered a valuable commodity to prospective students. In other words, can the school command high tuition and many applicants?

In fact, as a grim 1999 report from the University of Chicago attested, according to the university administration, this paragon of the vaunted Great Books curriculum was having trouble in its recruitment campaign precisely because, in opposition to the zeitgeist, it retained too much academic rigor. Consequently, the board and the administration announced a new emphasis away from its classical educational focus and toward a more lenient academic program, in addition to adding sports facilities and stronger placement services. Appalled members of the faculty and student body protested the shift, after which the university's president announced his resignation to take up teaching duties. But the board has neither retracted its program nor expressed any intention of modifying it. Despite the university's prestige, many on the faculty have discovered that even in matters of curriculum, the heart of faculty sovereignty, their powers are limited.

In the sciences, technologies, and graduate professional education, the two dozen or so leading public research universities are holding their own in this competition. Despite budget constraint imposed by state legislatures eager to reduce taxes for their business and upper-middle-class constituents, many have retained their ability to raise substantial research grants. For example, the University of California–Irvine and University of California–San Diego are major recipients of grants for bioengineering from agencies such as the National Institutes of Health and the Centers for Disease Control; Cornell, Berkeley, and Illinois are leading research institutions in physics; and Penn State and Pittsburgh are among the most important of the technical science research institutions. Where legislatures have cut back on operating funds, the proceeds from research activity often manage to keep programs in the humanities and arts alive.

The most severe problem institutions in public higher education are those in the tiers below the two categories of research universities. Apart from the departments and schools of teachers' education, which, though not prospering in this age of academic austerity, have substantial social utility, even by conservative lights, many universities and community colleges are scrambling to find a "mission" sufficiently attractive to convince skeptical legislators that they have an economically viable role. For the new mantra of higher education is that by training technically competent labor and also providing income to a large number of blue-collar, clerical, and professional workers, postsecondary schooling makes significant contributions to local and regional economies. Consequently, schools are making agreements with private corporations to provide curricula and teaching staff for dedicated skills training. Even when specific deals do not drive the curriculum, vocationalization does. As students get the message that in this global economy a higher-education credential is necessary for survival, many feel that they do not have the luxury of indulging their artistic, critical, or literary interests and must instead keep their collective noses to the technical grindstone. As a result, many social sciences departments are relegated to providers of "breadth" requirements or are encouraged or forced to adopt vocational majors in order to avoid being closed down. When majors have declined steeply, English departments have often become little more than composition mills.

For the time being, there is no imminent threat of school closings in most state systems. But university and college administrations in the third (nonresearch) tier are admonished by regents and state commissions of higher education to find ways to reduce budget shortfalls by raising tuition, making alliances with corporations or otherwise turning their predominantly liberal arts institutions into vocational schools, or adding more research capacity to their faculty and facilities. A history professor acquaintance tells me that the third-tier Illinois public university in which he teaches, once a broad general education school with a few scientific and technical programs, now consists largely of business and technical majors. Similar trends are evident in New York, New Jersey, Connecticut, Colorado, and California. The separation of their "flagship" schools and their largely undergraduate and master's-level institutions is widening. For the latter, the message is clear: Sink or swim. Needless to say, few administrators in public higher education are willing to risk the severe penalties of smaller enrollments and diminished income by retaining their liberal arts focus. The brute fact is that undergraduate humanities majors are few. Only in fields such as economics, because of its predominant business ties; political science, because it is understood as a good prelaw major; and sociology, because of the still lively interest in the social services as a profession, has there been some growth in student interest.

Even some private school students exhibit anxiety about the future; as we have seen, they are demanding better placement services and are sticking more closely to fields that have direct occupational outcomes rather than using their undergraduate schooling as a time of exploration and creative uncertainty. Some elite schools, public as well as private, remain beacons for English and other language majors, and some, such as Pittsburgh, have attractive undergraduate philosophy and history programs. But major state schools such as the four State University of New

York research universities, Rutgers, and many in the UC system report a decline in undergraduate majors in history, philosophy, and literature. Although most of these programs are in no imminent danger of becoming composition factories for technical majors and retain their highly rated PhD programs, the so-called economic boom has failed to produce a new era of relaxation. Students remain enervated because, I suspect, they know what the media have ignored: There is a lot of work but few jobs, if by jobs we designate work that is accompanied by the amenities of security, benefits, and a career ladder that enables them to gain income and authority along with experience. Moreover, they know from their own parents' experience that corporate downsizing affects middle management and professionals as well as blue-collar workers.

The economic and social environment of the late 1990s is inimical to the development of a system of public higher education in which the goals are defined beyond the utilitarian uses of credentials and acquisition of job skills. Many public colleges and universities are constituted as labor exchanges rather than public spaces where adults of all ages can take non-credit-bearing courses in world affairs as well as craft and art forms such as pottery, or participate in forums and conferences of all sorts. As for one of the historical aims of public higher education, the development of citizens able to participate in key decisions affecting the polity, this role has been consigned to one of the "distribution" requirements of the first two years of a baccalaureate degree. The hard fact is that continuing and citizenship education are now conceived of by administrators as moneymaking activities and are most effective in private institutions. Many threadbare public schools are bereft of these programs or offer only a limited range of skills-oriented courses.

III

With their victory in reimposing a core curriculum in most colleges and universities, education leaders in higher education are in the throes of a second stage of curriculum "reform," which has provoked considerable debate. The central issue is education for whom, and for what? The dispute over the curriculum takes many forms. Feminists and black, Asian, and Latino educators responded to the imposition of core curricula that resuscitated the traditional literary canon as a site of privileged learning by insisting on the inclusion of global, postcolonial, and otherwise marginalized literatures and philosophy. But the so-called multicultural or diversity curriculum only peripherally addresses the central problem that afflicts public universities: the command from executive authorities in and out of the institution that public schools justify their existence by proving value to the larger society (in most cases business interests). In turn, educational leaders such as presidents and provosts are inclined to seek a "mission" that translates as vocationalization, which entails leasing or selling huge portions of a school's curriculum and research products directly to companies.

As a result, the public research universities are dusting off one of Kerr's most important suggestions: Undergraduates as well as graduate students should be recruited to participate in the research activities of the professoriate, especially in the sciences. Now, like sports, research demands considerable time commitment from the practitioner. Some places, notably UC universities such as San Diego and Irvine, are reducing the obligation of science and technology majors to the humanities and social sciences so they can more accurately mimic the practices of the great private technical universities. This approach, of course, raises the question of whether the public universities as public goods should maintain their obligation to educate students in citizenship as well as in job skills.

In this connection, as a professor in UC Irvine's School of Social Sciences, I can recall legislative hearings in the 1970s conducted by the chair of the higher-education committee of the California State Assembly. The chair and other committee members were concerned that faculty were avoiding undergraduate teaching in the service of their research and that state universities were slighting programs aimed at educating for citizenship. The university administrators appeared to bow to the legislators' stern warning that if they did not alter the situation, their budgets would feel heat. But as with all attempts by legislatures to micromanage education, it did not take long for the administration and faculty to regain lost ground. Today most UC campuses are monuments to technoscience, and, with a few exceptions at the undergraduate level, the humanities and social sciences are gradually being relegated to ornaments and service departments.

In the third tier, the forms of privatization and vocationalization are far more explicit. For example, the New York telephone company Bell Atlantic (now Verizon) has developed relationships with public community and senior colleges throughout the state on the condition that the school agree to enroll and train students for specific occupations needed by the company. Although in most cases no money changes hands, the school benefits by additional enrollment and the college gains because it shows the legislature and other politicians that it is playing a role in increasing worker productivity and enhancing economic growth and for these reasons should be rewarded with funds. In addition to a degree, the employees learn occupational skills that often lead to upgrading, and the company transfers the costs of training it would have to do anyway to the public. Ironically, the Communications Workers of America (CWA), the collective bargaining representative, takes credit for the program by including the right of certain high-seniority members to an "education" in the contract—upgrading opportunities for which the CWA does not have to assume the cost of tuition.

The question at issue is whether schools should forge direct corporate partnerships and in effect sell their teaching staff, let alone the curriculum, to vocational ends. Needless to say, in the occupational programs I have examined, the liberal arts, especially English and history, play a service role; at Nassau Community College in Long Island students are required to take a course in labor history and their English requirement is confined to composition. The remainder of the two-year curriculum is devoted to technical subjects that are directly applicable to the telephone industry. Put more broadly, third-tier public colleges and universities are under pressure to reduce their humanities and social sciences offerings to introductory and service courses for the technical and scientific curriculum. In effect, the prospective English or sociology major faces a huge obstacle to obtaining a degree in the chosen discipline because there are often not enough courses to fulfill the major. As a result, we can observe the rush to mergers of social sciences departments in many third-tier public schools.

Sociology, anthropology, and political science departments are consolidating. At Cameron State University in Lawton, Oklahoma, by the early 2000s the two philosophers on campus were in the social science department, which includes the traditional disciplines and teaches courses such as business ethics. In order to maintain viability, the department has majors in occupational specializations such as the large major in social welfare—a vocational sequence designed to train counselors and low-level professionals in the criminal justice system, a thriving industry in the state. In the absence of a social and a political theorist, these required courses are taught by a criminologist. With almost 500 majors, the 11 full-time members of the department each teach more than 120 students in 4 course loads a semester, in addition to academic and professional advisement of bachelor's- and master's-degree students. Many courses are taught by adjuncts. Since the university has many business majors, a favorite program of dozens of third-tier schools, the humanities and social science departments are crucial for fulfilling the shriveling "breadth" requirements.

Economic pressures as much as the ideological assaults on the liberal arts account for the sea change in the curriculum that is in process in public higher education. As I have mentioned before, the student and her family feel more acutely the urgency of getting a leg up in the race for survival. The relative luxury of the liberal arts might be reserved for the few who are liberated from paid work during their college years. The consequence is that the human sciences are squeezed from the bottom as well as the top as students demand "relevance" in the curriculum and lose their thirst for reflection.

It may safely be declared that only in the larger cities, and then not uniformly, have faculty and students successfully defended the liberal arts. At CUNY a decade of determined faculty resistance has slowed, but not reversed, the trend. As the new century dawned, CUNY administrators were preparing their version of distance learning, one of the more blatant efforts to end the traditional reliance on classroom learning in favor of a model that focuses on the use of Internet technology to produce more standard packages of predigested knowledge. In addition, it is an answer to the fiscal crisis suffered by many public schools because the style of learning reduces the number and proportion of full-time faculty to adjuncts, transforms brick and mortar into cyberspace so that building and maintenance costs are reduced, and through standardization eliminates the mediation of a critical intellectual to interpret transmitted knowledge. The latter saving does not refer as much to cost as to the centralization of political and social control.

The bare fact is that neither the discourse nor the practices of critical learning are abroad in public higher education except as the rearguard protests of an exhausted faculty and a fragment of the largely demobilized student body. Blindsided by the 1960s rebellions, many educators went along with student demands for ending requirements and ended up with the marketplace in which demand-driven criteria determined curricular choices. In other words, neoliberalism entered the academy through the back door of student protest. Yet for progressive educators, the task remains: To demand a rigorous core of knowledges as a requisite of any postsecondary credential is today a radical act. For to capitulate to the "market"—which arguably wants something else because, in panic about an uncertain future, students and their parents really do not believe in the palaver of the "boom economy"—is to surrender the idea of higher education as a public good. Educators who would acknowledge that these institutions largely paid for by working-class and middle-class people should not promote critical thinking should not explore the meaning of citizenship in the new neoliberal era; they should abhor the project of democratic appropriation of both Western and subaltern (marginal) traditions through attitudes of bold skepticism.

Perhaps it is too early to propose that public higher education be thoroughly decommodified and shorn of its corporate characteristics, that all tuition costs be paid by a tax system that must be reprogressivized. Perhaps the battle cry that at least in the first two years only science, philosophy, literature, and history (understood in the context of social theory) be taught and learned and that specializations be confined to the last two years is so controversial, even among critics of current trends, that it remains too countercultural. Yet if higher education is to become a public good in the double meaning of the term—as a decommodified resource for the people and an ethically legitimate institution that does not submit to the business imperative—then beyond access we would have to promote a national debate about what is to be taught and what is to be learned if citizenship and critical thought are to remain, even at the level of intention, the heart of higher learning.

5

Subaltern in Paradise

In her widely disseminated article "Can the Subaltern Speak?" written more than twenty years ago, Gayatri Spivak urged her interlocutors to consider the condition of postcolonialism (Spivak 1988). Although so-called Third World nations are formally independent, their economies remained tied to global capitalism. And within these countries the poor, and especially women, remain silent and un- or underrepresented. In any case, they rarely represent themselves and remain under the domination of men, particularly their husbands and fathers. Spivak argued that Westerners cannot speak for those driven to silence by repression; despite good intentions, the ability of the poor to speak for themselves is hampered by liberal concern. Yet new struggles against global capitalism have produced a new discourse of human rights in which the universal has once more taken its place in the lexicon of emancipation. Spivak's admonition remains salient to our times, although it must be mediated by new conditions. People historically excluded from participation at any level of the national state must, in the end, engage in self-activity to overcome the burdens of domination and exploitation, but the repressive structures of state and patronal control, especially in rural areas of Asia, Africa, and Latin America, require a response from those privileged to acquire a global vision.

"Subalternity" is a euphemism for the excluded—the "other," the despised, the wretched of the earth. For better or for worse, the subaltern has been identified with the poor peasant classes, including the urban reserve army of labor, of what used to be termed "the Third World" and is now, more accurately, called "the developing world." In the so-called advanced capitalist societies (where the adjective refers to both the level of development of the forces of production and the generally high standard of living), we have been visibly touched by subaltern peoples due to the great waves of immigration that have been experienced by nearly all such societies. Like the immigration from eastern and southern Europe at the turn of the twentieth century, the current wave brings to the shores of the United States people who have been displaced from the land or, if urban dwellers, find themselves unable to earn a living. The United States is no longer the land of promise, but it still holds enough opportunity for people willing to work for sixty or seventy hours a week at substandard wages or maintain small businesses that serve the immigrant communities from which they themselves stem.

We are now engaged in a great international debate about immigration, a vital aspect of globalization. What is happening in Africa, China, India, and Latin America constitutes nothing short of new enclosures. As I reported in Chapter 3, hundreds of millions of people who once held some form of land tenure are being driven from the ancestral homes into the cities of the developing world and the developed world by the force of arms, law, technological innovation in agriculture, or hunger. There they find poorly paid industrial jobs and are condemned to casual labor—or none at all. Nor are they welcomed as potential citizens of their new habitats. Human rights advocates have argued that the old national boundaries are, to say the least, archaic. And the political economy of the developed world demands the importation of cheap, vulnerable labor to overcome the worldwide plague of falling rates of profit. Consequently, some argue that the movement of capital and, consequently, movements of labor across national borders make urgent a redefinition of citizenship. Many immigrants, especially in western Europe and Israel, have been classified as guest workers, a designation that subjects them to expulsion at any time. In developing countries they have little chance of attaining legal status.

Such disenfranchisement is not confined to immigrants. Despite their formal status as citizens within a nation-state, many native-born residents lack the basic elements of actual citizenship; they rarely, if ever, participate in the institutions of civil society such as parent-teacher associations, civic organizations, and trade unions. Even when they are employed, circumstances such as long working hours; multiple jobs; and, for women, the double shift conspire to exclude them from even the most informal institutions of democratic life. The United States, always the innovator in the abrogation of labor's rights—historically congealed not only in prohibitions of strikes and boycotts but also in the rank exclusion of blacks from the industrial workplace except in times of war—is a pioneer in introducing a new dimension of subalternity. Millions of workers, white as well as black, have been driven from the industrial workplaces, victims of the relentless cost-cutting policies of large and smaller corporations alike. Technological displacement, outsourcing, and capital flight have reduced the quantity and quality of industrial jobs. For example, faced with fierce global competition, mainly from developed societies, the once mighty and seemingly invulnerable U.S.-based car industry is shedding some of the best jobs, at least in monetary terms, in the American economy. The textile and apparel industries, once the largest employers of industrial labor, are a shadow of their former selves, having yielded to the blandishments of Latin America and East Asia—mostly China, whose wages are between 5 and 15 percent of its already low-wage U.S. counterparts. As the safety net rapidly disappears, laborers are forced into the informal economy—not only working off the books in industrial workshops but earning a living through such pursuits as drug dealing, prostitution, and other demeaning sources of contingent work.

But we are experiencing a new phase of subalternity. In nearly every sector of intellectual labor, a system has been constructed that establishes several classes within an increasingly clear hierarchy. From computer engineering and programming to academic labor, some are awarded "real" jobs while many are relegated to the status of part-time, contingent, and temporary labor. The computer professional is as likely to be a freelance repair and maintenance worker as a full-time employee. Like all freelancers, she has little time for recreation and certainly none for participation in the life of the community. Another case in point: Adjunct teachers in higher education are seldom anything but part-time workers. These positions are no longer filled by people whose day jobs in law, business, journalism, and highly specialized technical areas allow them to accept an occasional course when the host institution cannot afford to employ full-timers for courses best taught by experienced professionals who bring rich practical experiences to the classroom.

The new adjunct professor is likely to be a full-time wage slave whose teaching load exceeds that of a full-time tenured faculty member by two or three times. Teaching five to seven courses in two or three different institutions, the adjunct professor hardly has time for intellectual work, let alone for participation in political or civil society. These workers have become veritable prisoners of the flawed American dream: Get a good education (or at least a credential) and you can live the life of the mind, secure in your job, with full benefits and periodic sabbaticals for writing and spiritual refreshment. Instead they are situated at the bottom of the educational pyramid, and their lives consist of work without end. After more than a decade of fumbling, it appears that distance learning is regaining its legs. Given the systematic disinvestment currently globally rampant in higher education, one would expect new cost-cutting proposals to be put forward, often dressed in the garb of democratization. If this trend gains momentum, we may witness in our lifetimes an educational regime in which only a tiny minority of students and professors enjoy the luxury of classroom learning while the immense majority earns credentials without seeing a single live professor or conversing in person with fellow students. It will be the apogee of atomization of which classical sociological theory spoke at the turn of the twentieth century.

I

The twentieth-century history of American higher education was periodically punctuated by allegations that educational institutions had been seriously compromised by corporate and state influence in the conduct of academic inquiry and by administrative infractions against the traditional aspiration of shared governance. Thorstein Veblen's *The Higher Learning in America* (1993 [1918]) and Robert Lynd's *Knowledge for What?* (1964 [1939]) were prescient indictments of a not yet mature corporate university. Veblen's and Lynd's rants, asking whether higher learning should serve the public good or private gain, were regarded with considerable skepticism even as the authors were accorded the status of respected cranks. At the moments of their interventions, mainstream America was preoccupied with each of the two world wars and was seriously considering mobilizing its intellectual resources, including the universities. Under these circumstances, appeals to academic freedom and autonomy tended to fall on deaf ears. Indeed, President Franklin D. Roosevelt's science advisers recommended that a handful of elite public and private schools such as Berkeley and Princeton be charged with the responsibilities associated with scientific and technological aspects of the war effort, in contrast to some European countries where such research was conducted by independent institutes rather than universities. Although the decision was made to outsource the bulk of weaponry production to private firms rather than producing most materiel in government-owned plants (the atomic bomb was a major exception), the government remained the client of nearly all research products. Still, these wars and the Cold War that followed generated not only a massive arms industry but also the vast expansion and diversification of the chemical, electronics, and transportation industries, which were, collectively, the engines of economic expansion until the 1970s.

By 1960, under the imperatives of the Cold War, military and corporate power over nearly every aspect of U.S. society had so increased that no less a conservative than President Dwight D. Eisenhower warned against the "military-industrial complex," already discussed at great length by C. Wright Mills in his magisterial *The Power Elite* (Mills 1956). Veblen went so far as to argue that since the Morrell Act by which Congress for the first time had committed the federal government to support public higher education, primarily with land grants, the main business of the university was to provide knowledge and a trained cadre for private industry, especially the science and technology of agricultural production. The burden of his claim is that the concept of an autonomous university, revered since the Enlightenment, remained an ideal that was far from the existing situation. More than two years before the entrance of the United States into World War II changed the landscape of the relationship of higher education to the federal government, Lynd raised the disturbing question: Should the university serve the public rather than the private interest?

These were chiefly works of social criticism that pointed to corporatist tendencies within universities, even as most institutions of higher education promulgated the fiction that their faculty were dedicated to the disinterested pursuit of knowledge. Of course the decision of the Roosevelt administration, in the context of preparations for World War II, to invest its primary war research in a handful of leading universities had already raised doubts that scientists could remain free to perform their work independent of the influence of the military or the imperatives of the Cold War. Throughout the Cold War era, these doubts occupied the work of social critics and scholars such as I. F. Stone, Michael Klare,

Noam Chomsky, and Edward Herman. But the argument that the national security interests of the United States overrode concerns about their autonomy and the increasing centralization of funds for scientific and technological research in the military establishment persuaded many scientists to collaborate with the federal government's military program, especially because the Department of Defense provided significant support to basic research not directly linked to the war effort. One of the most important functions of these defense contracts was to support the university-based liberal arts, especially the humanities and social sciences. In fact, absent alternative sources of funds, national defense contracts were frequently the vehicle through which natural and social scientists were able to do theoretical research or work not directly connected to the war imperatives.

By the 1980s, writers such as Martin Kenney had discovered the "university corporate complex," focused not on government contracts but on university-business partnerships (Kenney 1986). In *Academic Capitalism,* Sheila Slaughter and Larry Leslie drew similar conclusions: The pursuit of knowledge as a public good, let alone for its own sake, was no longer a shared value of the academic community, if it ever had been (Slaughter and Leslie 1997). The collapse of the Soviet Union and the demise of its successor states as military superpowers and political rivals to the United States raised profound issues for the scientific establishment. How to sustain the high level of research within American universities in the post–Cold War era? Slaughter and Leslie's meticulous empirical research demonstrated that, in the wake of stagnation of federal financing of basic and applied research in the sciences in the 1980s and 1990s, leading research universities had added to their dependency by entering into "partnerships" with large pharmaceutical, chemical, and electronics corporations.

A 1992 conference attended by the presidents and other key officials of leading research universities was dedicated to responding to the challenge. According to conference organizer Jonathan Cole, Columbia University's provost, the universities had only one serious option: turning to private industry for support. Under these arrangements, corporations provided significant funds to the university in exchange for joint patents and "early access and review of all proposed publications and presentations by faculty members whose work the company supported" (Walsh 1994). Although research in the so-called policy sciences associated with branches of sociology and especially political science has not been as subject to direct corporate control and influence, these subdisciplines have long been adjuncts of the state (Fisher 1993). These relationships have prompted critics to ask whether the decline in terms of real dollars of the federal government's allocations to basic, disinterested research was a reflection of the conservative program of privatization of knowledge rather than budgetary constraints. Or, put another way, are the decades of "budget crisis" an ideological and political mask for an attack against public goods framed in purely fiscal terms?

The privatization of scientific knowledge has led to widespread secrecy. Scientists who otherwise would have unswervingly accepted the doctrine that it is in the nature of their work to share knowledge (the sociologist Robert Merton called it "communalism") were now, by contract, sworn to secrecy. The emergence of partnerships between the university and the corporations has had a chilling effect on the tradition of scientific transparency, shared knowledge, and open debate about new discoveries. It is not uncommon for presenters at scientific meetings to purge their papers of information that might violate the patent rights of their corporate sponsors. In addition, because the reward system of research universities is results-driven and, in a fiercely competitive global market, corporate partners demand that researchers keep ahead of the competition, the erosion of the ethic of honesty has led to frequent instances of fraud in reporting evidence. Some scientists have invested in or received lucrative consulting contracts from the corporations that support their research, often reaping substantial dividends. That such practices are condemned as unethical by leading spokespersons for the American Association for the Advancement of Science and other institutions is a measure of how widespread they are within scientific circles.

But there is barely a murmur about the underlying fact of the commodification of knowledge that has become the main consequence of the end of the bipolar world created by the Cold War. If knowledge is subject to market forces—that is, it can be bought and sold like any other commodity—what follows is that scientific knowledge has become private property and the research university is sustained by its ability to sell its wares to the highest bidder, in which case it becomes itself a corporate entity. Holding trade secrets is common practice among corporate competitors. But, in contrast with one of the first principles of the seventeenth-century scientific Enlightenment—that in the interest of encouraging criticism and revision, scientific knowledge be widely shared—commodification signifies the reverse: To the degree that the university remains a key producer of scientific knowledge, it may no longer be a bastion of open inquiry. Determining whether the subordination of knowledge to the commodity form is in the public interest is a complex question. If the fund of fundamental knowledge upon which technological innovation depends is deemed adequate for a multiplicity of applications, many corporations decide that a high volume of basic research is not only unnecessary but unproductive. Federal agencies such as the National Science Foundation may allocate some funds for these projects, but, absent a compelling case such as that provided by the race to develop nuclear weapons during World War II or during the Cold War, policy-makers have concurred with drug and electronics firms that new science must take a backseat to product development that can facilitate the investment, circulation, and profitability of capital. In short, as long as knowledge is viewed as a commodity, the concept of disinterest in research is bound to suffer eclipse.

II

Since the transformation of biology into a technoscience—where the fundamental molecular paradigm is intimately linked to applications—funds have become scarce for those who persist in working in the field of evolutionary science or in the old functionalist perspective. Today, if the university is not prepared to support such research, and private foundations, whose scientific sensibility is not far from the mainstream consensus, are not favorably inclined, the evolutionists as well as practitioners of some older biological disciplines find themselves without the laboratory facilities, travel funds, and assistants to facilitate their work. In the life sciences money is available virtually exclusively for research in molecular biology and biophysics, whose knowledge can be rapidly transformed in commercial biotechnological applications, especially for genetically modified organisms in food, and pharmaceuticals. These deprivations do not appear as a violation of academic freedom because no authority is telling biologists they cannot engage in the fascinating work associated with finding the origin of our species or of any other more than physicists are prohibited from addressing the building blocks of matter or the history of the universe. However, if money is no longer available save for a tiny corps of investigators, the priorities themselves are tantamount to refusing such projects, and scientists who wish to stay "relevant" are well advised to fall into line.

Perhaps the most serious challenge to the independence of the academic system of American society is the effect of these practices upon the most fundamental right still possessed by the professoriate: academic freedom. Since the Clinton administration, federal science policy has encouraged dedicated rather than basic research. The fact that federal agencies such as the National Science Foundation and the National Institutes of Health charged with dispensing research funds have increasingly privileged proposals "dedicated" to producing knowledge that can be readily translated into products is by now almost commonplace. The relative decline of funding for theoretical physics, for example, may be attributed to the long period of transition between basic science and practical consequences. Some apologists for the current policy have argued that we have arrived at the "end" of physics: There are no basic truths to be discovered, only a few glitches to be cleaned up. This is, of course, a parallel argument to the end-of-history thesis advanced most famously by Francis Fukuyama (Fukuyama 1992). In neither sphere is the argument true, even if, in the current conjuncture of idealess science and social science, it "feels" true.

Of course, during the period of war emergency (not yet ended), the federal government, in the interest of national security, claims the right to establish priorities in scientific research and deploys fiscal incentives to enforce its position. This approach is particularly effective at a time when the costs of scientific research, specifically in technology needed to perform experiments, lead to the distinction between "big" science and "little" science. The exemplars of big science are well known: groups engaged in applications of physics and engineering to space travel; the huge accelerators needed for experiments in high-energy particle physics; the massive biophysics programs at the Massachusetts Institute of Technology and at various University of California (UC) campuses, especially Berkeley, Davis, San Diego, Irvine, and Santa Barbara. But even at centers of so-called little science such as New York's Mount Sinai School of Medicine, where during the 1980s the focus was sharply limited to finding molecular biological solutions to problems of brain research, funding opportunities drove the research program of the entire school. There is no reason to believe that any significant research institution today would take a different approach. Under such circumstances, leading theoretical physicists such as the late Richard Feynman or Steven Weinberg or evolutionists and biologists such as the late Stephen J. Gould and Richard Lewontin are important to the university as ornaments signifying its commitment to intellectual excellence. Meanwhile, most of the work that the university needs for its financial sustenance gets done in the knowledge factories of lucrative research.

But with rewards go punishments. Immediately after September 11, 2001, among many other reconfigurations of civil liberties and academic freedom, the Bush administration launched a program of harassment of professors, mainly those of Middle Eastern background, who were not U.S. citizens. Some state universities collaborated with the Justice Department by dismissing these professors or permitting the government to implement a program of surveillance. The government justified these serious acts of political repression on national security grounds; as a result, save for the objections registered by human rights and civil liberties organizations, they went largely unchallenged. More recently, again on the pretext of national security, the administration floated a proposal to enable the federal government to intervene more directly in monitoring curricula offered by American universities to foreign students. A recent case at the prestigious UC-Berkeley raises far more serious issues for our conceptions of the core mission of higher education. In fall 2003 the university administration denied tenure to Ignacio H. Chapela, an assistant professor of ecology, overriding his department's unanimous recommendation and that of the faculty senate to grant him tenure. In November 2001 Chapela and a graduate student, David Quist, had published an article in the British science journal *Nature* that "claimed that native corn in Mexico had been contaminated by material from genetically modified corn." Six months later the journal received a number of letters contesting the research, and the journal issued an editorial note stating that the evidence was not "sufficient to justify the original paper." As the controversy brewed, Chapela said he suspected the journal had been pressured by scientists working with the biotechnology industry and noted that he had been a critic of a 1998 deal between UC-Berkeley and Norvartis, a Swiss biotechnology company, in which the university receives $5 million each year for five years "in exchange for early review of all proposed publications and presentations by faculty members whose work the company supported" (Walsh 1994).

The Chapela affair is only one of the more blatant instances in which the administration of a leading research university has been strongly suspected of invoking nonacademic criteria in order to turn down a candidate for tenure. During the 1960s academic dissent was frequently met by university authorities with retributive contempt. Although some stood up to government pressure to discipline recalcitrant professors, Columbia University's administration took pains to create an inhospitable environment so that even some prominent tenured professors felt obliged to leave. At the same time, it became an open secret that after 1968, when the entire campus was rife with student demonstrations, the administration, which held the right to grant tenure tightly in its hands, routinely denied that status to radicals, even as it claimed that it was free of prejudice because most assistant professors were denied tenure. Of course, the principle and practice of academic freedom are at the heart of this matter. But alongside the capacity of the institution to tolerate criticism, especially of its own corporate relationships, lurks the long-contested issue of the role of the faculty in academic governance at a time when higher education is increasingly privatized. During the past fifteen years, the professoriate has stood by as the allegiances of administration have, with the encouragement of state governments, shifted from a commitment to higher education as a "public good" to becoming contract players in the theater of capitalist hegemony. With the exception of a few relatively privileged departments and elite institutions, the humanities and social sciences have suffered near-crippling cuts or stagnation even as science and technology programs are funded in order to prepare them to seek private money.

Chapela's tenure case was at first hardly controversial, either in his own department or at the level of the faculty as a whole. That the administration made the decision to override a consensual judgment of his peers underscores a problem that has bedeviled advocates of what has been termed "shared governance" for decades. Although they have acknowledged the governing role of university administration—mistakenly, I would argue—they have insisted on the equal role of the faculty, especially in academic matters such as tenure and promotion. Indeed, the establishment of promotion and tenure committees, which, in most instances, are composed exclusively of peers, perpetuates the perception of shared governance. Yet in all public universities and colleges and the large majority of private institutions, decisions of promotion and tenure committees and deans have the standing of being recommendations to a sovereign administration, which may with impunity turn down the recommendations of lower bodies. In fact, the arbitrary authority of the president and his or her office is frequently challenged by candidates, faculty senates, and unions. Many schools have established appeals tribunals that hear cases of faculty discharge, discrimination in salary issues, and refusal of tenure and promotion. In some schools where unions have bargaining rights, such cases may be subject to a formal grievance procedure. But in many instances, candidates are obliged to go to court in order to obtain restitution—and in general, courts are extremely reluctant to intervene in what they believe are purely academic decisions.

The broad application of tenure, won after decades of agitation and struggle, signifies that the faculty is free to pursue channels of inquiry that may be unpopular and unprofitable for the university and its partners—but there is reason to believe that its short sixty-year reign is under siege. That both public and private universities and colleges have, in the wake of budget constraints and their own priorities, adopted the practice of employing adjuncts and graduate students to teach the bulk of introductory courses is fairly well known. Many adjuncts are superb teachers. In any case, they are often no worse than the full-time faculty. In pedagogical terms, the difference resides primarily in the fact that the part-timer is rarely paid for the time required for student academic advisement or for class preparation. Beyond these egregious conditions, the spread of a vast contingent workforce in academe threatens both tenure and academic freedom. It undermines tenure because the overwhelming majority of part-time adjuncts are hired by the semester or by the academic year; the condition of their reappointment militates against their participation in free intellectual inquiry. Lack of freedom may be ascribed not so much to policy as to their uncertain situation. Any conflict with a department chair—personal, intellectual, or political—can be, and often is, an occasion for termination of even a long-standing relationship with the institution. And many schools have recently hired faculty on one- to five-year non-tenure-track contracts, some of which are renewable at the discretion of the administration, others not. At Harvard, Yale, and other elite institutions, these appointments may become stepping-stones to permanent jobs elsewhere. However, in ordinary third-tier four-year colleges and universities, faculty members often migrate to another temporary assignment after finishing their stint.

We are at the beginning of an era in which tenure is rapidly becoming a privileged status reserved for a relatively small minority of faculty. When this or the next generation of tenured faculty retires from active service, unless the professoriate as a collective entity is better organized and mobilized than at present, we may experience a return to the situation that prevailed from the nineteenth century through the first five decades of the twentieth century. At that time, tenure was only rarely granted by boards of trustees at private institutions, and the situation was no better at public colleges and universities. For example, Lionel Trilling, one of the leading literary scholars and critics of the post–World War II period, received tenure at Columbia after more than ten years on one-year contracts during which he held the rank of instructor despite having earned a PhD and published a major biography of Matthew Arnold as well as innumerable articles in leading cultural journals. Similarly, although one or two professors in Columbia's anthropology department were tenured, important figures such as Ruth Benedict and Margaret Mead never held permanent positions, a testament to the sexism that pervaded that institution prior to the rise of second-wave feminism.

The presumption of tenure for qualified scholars and intellectuals was achieved by determined and dogged advocacy by the small but prominent American Association of University Professors (AAUP). Founded in 1915 as a national organization dedicated to academic freedom at a moment when college and university presidents—most of whom were politically conservative—wielded almost unlimited power, the AAUP had three key objectives: the institution of tenure for all qualified faculty, the ability of faculty to engage in free inquiry and speak and write dissenting opinions without facing discharge and other forms of discrimination, and shared governance. Although the association's efforts were crucial in the post–World War II adoption and routinization of tenure by most schools, fears of a postwar recession must be awarded equal credit. Some 1.5 million students attended institutions of higher education in 1941; nine years later the number had doubled, largely due to the enactment by Congress in 1944 of the Servicemen's Readjustment Act (popularly known as the GI Bill of Rights) that sanctioned tuition-free school attendance for returning veterans and provided them with financial support and housing during the transition between service in the armed forces and paid work. It was, next to Social Security, the most comprehensive New Deal reform.

The Cold War was no less beneficial to higher education. The dramatic increase of enrollments combined with federal funding through the Department of Defense for student loans as well as graduate assistantships continued almost unabated for twenty-five years until the end of the Vietnam War. From the Depression era, when the relatively small number of teachers with PhDs constituted a glut on the academic market, to the first twenty years after World War II, during which graduate programs expanded as fast as they had public funds to do so but were still woefully behind the demand—according to a popular saying, all one needed to get an academic teaching job was a PhD and a heartbeat—many academic institutions hastened to institute tenure, chiefly to attract qualified applicants. Although pay was modest, at least in comparison to other opportunities for educated workers in the rapidly expanding service and industrial sectors, the prospect of lifetime job security was attractive to many who still had vivid memories of Depression hardships and may have experienced the effects of the postwar recessions of 1954, 1958, and 1960–1961.

Only the rise of academic unionism from the late 1960s through the 1980s, a period that witnessed the organization of more than 30 percent of faculty and staff in colleges and universities, and growing enrollments, which increased by a factor of 500 percent from 1950 to 2000, temporarily saved tenure from a powerful counterattack. Yet as many institutions, beleaguered by fiscal constraint and shifting priorities, met their curricular and pedagogical needs in the human sciences with part-time and contingent labor, the routine practice among nonelite institutions of granting tenure to faculty who met certain informal publication, teaching, and service requirements came under scrutiny. Of course the claim of some educational economists and leaders of academic disciplines that graduate schools had saturated the "market" by overproducing PhDs was a fallacy born of their naive acceptance of administrative claims. If the constituents of the higher-education industry had insisted that colleges and universities replace retirees, the deceased, and others who left university employment on a one-to-one basis; indexed the number of full-time hires to enrollments; and enforced limits on faculty-student ratios, we might still suffer from a continuing shortage in some fields. In any case, the concept of glut is a corporate ideological construct whose success is attributable not to natural "market" causes but to the prevailing relationship of political forces within the academy. If "the handwriting is on the wall," it is not fated to come to pass. As long as professors refuse to deconstruct the ideology of overproduction, they are likely to transfer blame from the institution to themselves. In the beleaguered disciplines of language study, emulating the building trades, prominent professors began to call for limiting the supply of PhDs by raising admissions standards, or, as two progressives argued, institutionalizing a two-tier professoriate by establishing a special "teaching" credential (Berube and Nelson 1994).

III

Why has the collective higher-education administration been so compliant with pressures to join the mainstream of the U.S. labor market in the relentless drive toward casualization of a considerable fraction of academic labor.? After all, most middle-level administrators and top officials were and are recruited from the professorial ranks despite a powerful push from a variety of sources to install high-level corporate bureaucrats in leading academic administrative positions. The common explanation for the capacity of administrators to adjust to the new market-driven realities of their "industry" relies heavily on two detours from the historical experience of expanded public funding. Under the weight of federal and state tax cuts and recessionary conditions that combined to reduce state revenues, state legislatures throughout the 1980s and 1990s (which were years of official prosperity) sharply reduced funding for education as a whole. Particularly in the Northeast and on the West Coast, they were especially harsh on state colleges and universities. In the past three years, even some Southern and historical Midwestern land-grant universities, which were previously protected by the fact that many legislators are their graduates, have suffered some funding cuts. According to this wisdom, higher education got a bad name because of student and faculty dissent from the 1960s to the present but began to suffer when many state governments were captured by the Right. Under these conditions, it is argued, administration, which is, after all, a professional bureaucracy and not a political party, has little choice but to adjust its strategies to the new realities—privatization of the sciences and technologies; the outsourcing of many services such as building maintenance, food service, and bookstores; and unrelieved cost-cutting in the least economically viable branches such as the arts, humanities, and "soft" social sciences (for example, anthropology), which do not raise large amounts of outside money.

To these I would add a third transformation, which helps explain why we have seen so little resistance within the top echelon of administrators. Historically, presidents, provosts, and deans were, and still are, recruited mainly from faculty ranks and accepted these posts as an entailment of academic citizenship. After six or at most nine or ten years, they looked forward to returning to the ranks of the professoriate. If they were serious intellectuals—scholar, social critic, or scientist—administration was considered a "duty," like the armed services, not a career. However, with the advent of the corporate university, teaching and research are now regarded by many as a prelude to a much more lucrative career as an administrator. The corporatization of the academy requires the formation of a cadre whose loyalty is no longer to its erstwhile colleagues whose main duties are teaching, research, and writing but to the new institutional mission of making the university relevant to the dominant forces within the political economy. The measure of a successful administrative career is no longer academic leadership; indeed, many deans and presidents seem curiously indifferent to what goes on in the classroom or in the public life of the college or university. What counts is the size of the endowment; the quantity of research funds; and, in the public universities, success in holding the line against legislative budget cuts.

How to consolidate a "team" at the top of the corporate university whose loyalty is firmly ensconced in the institution and its corporate partners? The major requirement is to reconfigure the institution on the model of the American corporation. The corporate hierarchy has a chain of command in which, in contrast to the old collegial university or even the small family firm, the boundaries between executives and line employees is fairly rigid and the division between intellectual and manual labor is strictly enforced. In the private corporation, these tiers are rarely porous. Executives are rarely recruited from the professional ranks, and manual workers may rise only to the level of line supervision. As previously mentioned, the trend in colleges and universities is to recruit presidents and vice presidents of finance, administration, and other posts from the ranks of corporate chief executive, financial, and operating officers or top military commanders. In the old regime, presidents who came from the teaching ranks might earn as much as 50 percent over their base pay, but search committees cannot offer such pittances to CEOs, CFOs, and generals. The solution, gradually put in place over the past decade or so, has been the executive pay plan.

This plan replaces the former practice of offering a 50 percent stipend to the president and 10–25 percent stipends over their professorial pay to vice presidents, deans, and provosts, an increase that terminates when they return to the academic ranks. Now the president is considered to be a CEO, and, as university executives and corporate executives have become increasingly interchangeable, his or her salary tends to become more competitive, although by no means identical to that of a similar position in private industry. In 2004 some presidents of leading universities were earning $500,000 to $750,000 a year plus stipends for housing, a car and driver, and unlimited travel. In addition, many of them sit as paid directors of corporate boards—even for those corporations with which the university has relationships. These boards are often quite remunerative, bringing the president's income above $1 million a year. The sticky position is the academic affairs vice president or provost for which tradition still demands a genuine academic. But the executive pay plan for the top academic officers tends to separate them from the professorial ranks. It is not uncommon for provosts and academic vice presidents in private universities to earn twice the top rate of the elite professoriate or three times the median rate of the full-time faculty. At most public universities, the ratio of provosts' to top professors' pay has risen to 1.5 to 1. It is not likely that these individuals would appreciate term limits, or, more to the point, look forward to returning to the classroom.

What has resulted from the adoption of the corporate model for higher education? The interests of the institution are now everywhere separate from those of the collegium, and we have seen the formation of a professional managerial class whose relationship to the intellectual life of the institution is increasingly remote or, to be more exact, tends to reduce faculty and staff to employees in both the private and public sectors. The administration is charged with "management," not merely of buildings and grounds, services and finances, but also of its core activities: teaching and learning. In many of the 4,200 institutions of postsecondary education, provosts, under presidential direction, no longer depend on faculty initiatives to undertake innovative programs or devise new curriculum. "Academic planning" has become the province of the administration, and, under the rubric of "service to the university," faculty members are invited—or assigned—to do the basic work needed to put administrators' ideas into practice. At the community colleges, which enroll half of all students in postsecondary learning, mandates from above ordinarily entail prescription of certain textbooks and even pedagogies. Since many two- and four-year degree programs are undertaken in partnership with private corporations, the curriculum may be packaged by the company. In this case, the faculty is relegated to transmitter of received knowledge, which is no longer a symbolic act but becomes a literal mandate.

In first- and second-tier research institutions, top officials, ever sensitive to market forces, have embarked on a determined effort to recruit nationally recognized scholars. Given the exigencies of public finance, many public universities find themselves outbid by the leading private institutions, whose endowments and investments enable them to attract the top talent. Consequently, the privileged few among the professoriate are in a position to earn salaries that are double the median salaries of even the highest-paid at these institutions. For example, while in 2004 full professors at Columbia, Yale, and Harvard earned an average annual salary in the range of $125,000 to $150,000, it is not uncommon for superstars in the humanities or social and natural sciences to enter these universities at a salary of $250,000 plus generous travel funds, housing allowances, and funding for several assistants. In some instances, their teaching loads are half those of the average faculty member. The small circle of superstars tends to regard its appointments as sinecures from which to pursue their private interests. Some continue to perform research and writing, and others become public figures. But, with exceptions, they remain fairly remote from the festering problems of their own universities: They stand idly by while graduate assistants struggle for better pay and benefits; they are often impervious to the fate of their less-anointed colleagues whose salaries have remained relatively stagnant for years; and they tend to ally themselves with administration in struggles over faculty governance. Needless to say, few are in contact with undergraduates, and they have few ideas about education.

IV

The late Jacques Derrida issued a strong but gentle plea to protect and defend academic freedom and the autonomy of the university against the nefarious consequences of corporate takeover and the consequent subordination of academic knowledge to private interests. To these threats we have added the dangers of the formation of a distinct administrative class whose economic and ideological interests are tied to the corporate order and of an increasingly intrusive state in everyday academic affairs, especially abrogating a faculty's control over hiring, tenure and promotion, curricular matters, and its own production of knowledge. But we have learned that the American system of higher education has been, for almost 150 years, partially integrated into the state and, as if to belie its image of an ivory tower, a practical adjunct to the scientific and technological basis of both the production and administration of things as well as people.

If these theses are true—and one's evaluation will depend almost entirely on her or his standpoint—the task of preserving, let alone restoring, what remains of academic freedom is nothing less than monumental. Plainly, the starting point must be to challenge the professoriate to recognize the assault upon free inquiry; the autonomy of the faculty as a collectivity; and its most powerful weapons, especially tenure. Those who would defend academic freedom are obliged to recognize that a substantial portion of the faculty has been so bludgeoned by recent developments that it has lost hope. Another, much smaller segment may be afflicted with unease at the measure of how much faculty members have become complicit with corporate and government funders who dictate the nature and direction of much scientific research, including most of the social scientific disciplines and education. A third group lacks all reflexivity because it has been formed in the era when the concept of partnership—read faculty subordination to corporate control—seems a thing of nature and, more to the point, the royal road to academic and financial reward.

Who is left? Philosophers (mostly not in philosophy departments, especially in the research universities), social theorists, "humanists," unrepentant liberals and radicals, and a tiny fraction of libertarians who bridle at corporatization because they realize that it has little to do with the free market. Many are to be found in faculty senates and councils, among academic union activists and the tiny band of public intellectuals. Needless to say, in the main, their voices remain muted in the avalanche of crises that have afflicted higher education. If Derrida's call to arms is to be heeded, his interlocutors will require strategic acumen to enter the fray. Where to start will depend on what issues arouse a powerful minority to focused outrage.

The experience of social movements, especially the labor movement, tells us that the grievances that will induce a group to take action are, from the standpoint of analysis, often not the most consequential. At a time of war mobilization, faculty members may not pay heed to the blatant violations of the rights of alien professors and, under pressure of fiscal constraint, may shrug off the evidence of creeping privatization. But will they rationalize administrative refusal to heed faculty recommendations for tenure and promotion? They might take umbrage at administrators who never tire of invoking the doctrine of sacrifice in a time of emergency, treating themselves to huge salaries while imposing salary freezes on faculty and staff and relentlessly pursuing the program of casualizing large chunks of the teaching labor force. At public universities and colleges, they might bridle at the state's effort to subvert the faculty's prerogatives by imposing mandates—funded as well as unfunded—on the curriculum. In short, what will get the professoriate to act is impossible to determine in advance. But one thing we do know: The more abstract the appeal, the least likely it is to provoke practical activity. Phrases such as "academic freedom," "corporate university," and "shared governance" retain ideological resonance. More difficult is to find the concrete instances by which these ideals are violated. Such is the task of a good organizer.

As the Swedish writer and ethnographer Goran Palme once claimed, we must "dig where we stand." In solidarity, progressives and radicals have an obligation to support struggles against global capital, racism, and violence perpetrated against women wherever they are called to action. Acts of solidarity in one place, especially in the advanced industrial societies, only strengthen the movement of the subaltern everywhere. But the real test of a determined struggle for freedom and democracy is whether intellectuals and activists are prepared to fight to preserve and to establish the elements of citizenship in their own communities and institutions. For in the final accounting, the assault against the subaltern is directly proportional to the level of understanding and mobilization in both the developed and the developing world that they share a common foe: global capital. The precipitous decline of the labor movements and political forces of opposition in all western European countries and those of North America has largely left peoples in the developing world to fend for themselves. Whether they can secure survival and advancement alone is doubtful. But the chief obstacles to the emergence of a truly transnational movement to match transnationalization of capital reside right here.

If we understand the concept of the subaltern in a new way—as a concept that not only calls attention to the situation of economic deprivation but describes the absence of social and political freedom—then there is a basis for rescuing the movements for solidarity with the "other" from the throes of abstract moralism and achieving our own freedom. It is true that our condition of servitude is, even after more than thirty years of deterioration of living standards for most workers in advanced capitalist countries, more subtle and elusive. Among other things, we have a substantial professional managerial class, of which large sections of the professoriate are part. And there is a loose and ultimately disastrous credit system to sustain many over the bumps of frictional unemployment, steep deductibles for health care, and the high costs of energy and postsecondary education of our children or ourselves. Many of us have become so accustomed to defeat that we have come to believe that domination and subordination are inherent human conditions. We becomes bystanders in our own oppression and, in the wake of global warming, which threatens the very existence of life on the planet, fret rather than take decisive action.

We can no longer be content to repeat the outworn truism that living standards, even for the poor, are much higher in the West than elsewhere. For those suffering the insecurities of the new restructuring of labor conditions, and those who have witnessed the erosion of their capacity to play a crucial role in the governance of society in general and their own neighborhoods, cities, states, and workplaces in particular, to be reminded of relative privilege is neither solace nor an incentive to action. For people engage in acts of solidarity only when their own situation is being addressed by collective organization and action. Higher education is no exception. If current arrangements continue, all but a tiny minority will be rendered subaltern. And if that occurs, the whole promise of education as the road to freedom will have been crushed.

◇

6

Academic Unionism and the Future of Higher Education

In spring 1969 I was asked to come to Madison to meet with the leadership of a new Teaching Assistants Association (TAA) at the University of Wisconsin and address a meeting of its membership. I suppose the invitation had to do with two of my preoccupations at the time. Throughout the 1960s I had been a full-time union official, first for the Amalgamated Clothing Workers (now UNITE) and then for the Oil, Chemical, and Atomic Workers, where I directed organizing for the northeast district.

My other credential was in the antiwar movement. I was a columnist for the *Guardian,* then the preeminent newspaper of the New Left, and, as a leader of the movement (in 1965 I had co-organized the first national coordinating committee against the war) (see Aronowitz 1984, 1996), during the previous year I had been asked to debate the assistant secretary of state for Southeast Asia affairs, Roger Hilsman, on the occasion of the centennial of the University of Wisconsin. Maybe five thousand students and faculty, most of them war opponents, heard me rail against the war. Hilsman, a very nice person, had to carry the water for the Johnson administration's unpopular policy in one of the strongholds of the opposition. I did not have to be particularly effective to win the day.

The two thousand or so graduate teaching assistants wanted help from a quarter other than the official labor movement, which, in 1969, was riven over the war question as well as many other issues. As a known independent labor radical with strong ties to the student movement, I could be trusted, even though I was over thirty. What I had to say was far less important than the fact of the close connection between a new social movement and trade union-ism, a connection that accounts, in my opinion, for the startling and largely unexpected rise of unionism among public employees and professionals—doctors, attorneys, as well as professors and other teachers—in the same period. Among the forgotten stories of the much-celebrated and excoriated 1960s was the explosive growth of public employee unionism and the birth of a new era of professional unionism as well. By 1975 about four million public and service employees had joined unions, the same number as the far more heralded movement of industrial workers in the late 1930s (Aronowitz and DiFazio 1994). While the thirty years since the mid-1960s was a period of decline for the independent profes-sional and, for professors, a period of steady proletarianization, it was also a moment that witnessed the explosive power of the femi-nist, civil rights, and antiwar movements to change the culture of American life. Nearly all of the new union leaders associated with this "white-collar" movement were sympathizers with, when not active participants in, these social movements. This is true of the teachers even though the New York local—then more than now the heart of the national organization—was led by staunch defenders of the administration and its foreign policy (those union members in New York were largely indifferent to feminism but were actively engaged in mainstream civil rights struggles).

The modern labor movement was born in the turmoil of mass immigration, much of which was destined to fill the industrial plants of the Northeast and the Midwest. From 1880 to 1920, organized workers—skilled and unskilled—fought for a measure of industrial democracy and social justice *both* as newly arrived immigrants and as laborers. While the post–Civil War labor move-ment had been dominated by native-born craftsmen, the AFL (American Federation of Labor), still a craft-dominated movement, was led by Irish and German immigrants who were acutely aware of ethnic discrimination as much as class exploitation. The great (defeated) Homestead Strike (1892) is exemplary of the combina-tion of efforts by traditional craftspeople to protect their gains in the wake of encroaching industrialism and the yearning of unskilled Eastern European immigrant workers for social justice. The turn of the century was marked by the rise of the Jewish Labor Movement and the struggles of Italian and Polish textile workers, miners, and steelworkers for a union (Krause 1992).

Seen in the perspective of the unfulfilled promise of immi-gration, even the industrial uprisings of the 1930s cannot be viewed as a pure class movement. While the auto industry was, together with electrical production and oil refining, among the first industries in which the workforce was mainly native-born, steel, mining, textiles, and the needle trades were still bastions of foreign-born labor and, in the case of steel, blacks.

W. E. B. Du Bois declared the color line to be the defining social question of the twentieth century (Du Bois 1903). Indeed, from the standpoint of black labor, even the CIO (Congress of Industrial Organizations) drive with its pledge of complete equality did not erase the exclusionary practices of the postreconstruction industrial era. The period between 1935 and 1955, when industrial unionism was at its peak, was filled with struggles against discrimination within the unions as well as the companies. To this day, blacks have not been fully integrated into industrial crafts such as those practiced by tool and die workers, machinists, and electricians. The color line persists, and it is virtually impossible to write a history of the labor movement in this century without placing the race question at the center (Lichtenstein 1996, 374 and passim).

Although the emergence of the feminist movement in the 1960s may be ascribed, in the main, to a cultural rebellion against the traditional woman's role as wife, homemaker, and exclusive child-rearer, one of its notable consequences was that when women marched out of the kitchen and into the paid workforce, they discovered that "women's" jobs paid less than those of men in union as well as nonunion workplaces and that women suffered poor working conditions and little job protection in the factory and clerical workplace. To protest these conditions without collective action invited harassment and discharge.

One may conjecture that these injustices, long festering in public employment, health care, teaching, and social work, suddenly came to the surface in hospitals, social welfare agencies, and schools, just as the U.S. post office, where blacks were able to get jobs because much of the work was underpaid, became a hotbed of unionism in part because of the emergence of race politics in the 1960s. Even as most unions in production industries were beginning to witness membership erosion due to technological change and "runaway" shops in the late 1960s, public employees' unions were flourishing.

Of course, union growth in the public and nonprofit workplaces was spurred by relatively prolabor national administrations in the 1960s; in 1962, President Kennedy signed a landmark executive order introducing collective bargaining for federal employees. But, although state and local governments outside southern and other blatantly antiunion states followed with similar laws and administrative edicts, these prolabor gestures did not result in automatic success. New York social service employees conducted two major strikes during this period; teachers' strikes spread from the groundbreaking New York 1964 walkout to other parts of the country, and many of the movement's leaders went to prison for their defiance of state statutes barring public employee strikes; hospital worker strikes were a commonplace of the decade, especially among the lowest-paid workers (those in the patient care, dietary, and housekeeping categories), most of whom were women—and in the big cities, they were largely black and Latino (Fink and Greenberg 1989).

The turn-of-the-century battles of garment workers for decent wages and working conditions coincided with the first wave of feminism—the struggle for the vote and for birth control. Thus, needle-trades unions, once dominated by craftsmen, were obliged and able to address the needs of a growing female workforce as most other male-dominated unions were not. The famous "uprising of the twenty thousand," marking the emergence of mass needle-trades unionism following the Triangle Shirtwaist fire, was a movement of women against sweatshop conditions suffered largely by women. Similarly, more than fifty years later Hospital Workers Local 1199 and the American Federation of State, County, and Municipal Employees (AFSCME) translated the struggle for equality into a fight for women's and blacks' equality on the job. In contrast to the usual economistic appeals of industrial and craft unions, public and health care unionism wrapped themselves in the iconography of the feminist and civil rights movements.

Martin Luther King Jr. became the willing patron saint of the hospital workers' campaign, and many AFSCME affiliates established women's committees, promoted women to middle and high union positions, and developed strategies for dealing with wage inequality between women and men. One of these strategies was to reevaluate "women's" jobs upward by introducing the concept of "comparable worth," which analyzed male and female jobs according to the same criteria and which struck terror into the hearts of politicians and public sector bureaucrats until a series of court decisions slowed and ultimately defeated the movement.

The concept of comparable worth stems from the widely accepted tenet of "equal pay for equal work." Because few women have the same jobs as men, however, this popular principle does little to advance women's interests. Comparable worth advocates argue that the principle should be extended, as objective measures show that women's jobs are underpaid compared to the equivalent male jobs (Blum 1991).

At the time of the TAA fight for recognition at the University of Wisconsin, academic unionism, among faculty as much as among students, was a relatively rare phenomenon. Although the American Federation of Teachers (AFT) had a number of small locals of college and university teachers, almost none of them had yet won collective bargaining in matters pertaining to salaries, workloads, and benefits. Academic unionism, like teacher unionism generally, was still at the lobbying stage; state legislatures and city councils were the main arena for winning more money for teacher salaries. TA unionism was virtually unheard of.

Indeed, when I arrived at Madison, the TAA officers were still unsure of their ground. They had managed to recruit the vast majority of the TAs, but they were not at all confident that the university administration would recognize them as bargaining agents. The administration made now-familiar arguments against TA unionism: the TAs' teaching duties were part of their academic program as *students*; in effect they were professors "in training," not employees. They received grants, not salaries.

The TAs were concerned with workload as well as income issues; from their point of view, they were part of the instructional staff of the institution and enjoyed few of the perks of privileged graduate students in the natural sciences. Far from being apprentices, many handled classes with almost no supervision: They prepared lessons, provided undergraduates with academic counseling, and, in the aggregate, accounted for a considerable portion of undergraduate teaching. When not delivering lectures to large assemblages, the professoriat was busy performing the research activities for which they were rewarded. For the typical tenured professor at such a university, undergraduate teaching was a nuisance when not an actual impediment to professional advancement.

By 1969, it was already clear to most English, philosophy, and history graduate students that the job market had tightened, and, except for economists, whose job prospects did not really dim until the great downsizing of the 1990s, social scientists, if not natural scientists, were beginning to feel the pinch as well. While jobs in research universities were available for some, perhaps a majority of those trained in the humanities could look forward to teaching in a small state school or a community college or, worse, becoming part of the academic proletariat of temporary, part-time, and contingent adjunct instructors. A few years later, the full-time job had all but disappeared in history and philosophy; English was making its long march from literary to composition studies, and only those attached to well-known national figures in their respective fields could expect to obtain a research university job—and even then they were often hired not to teach literature but to direct composition programs.

At the same time, university administrations were solving the problem of expanding undergraduate enrollments not primarily by hiring new full-time faculty but by increasing class size in lower-division courses and pressing TAs to teach sections of fifty students or more. My son, who entered Rutgers University in 1971, told of attending three-hundred-student lower-division courses addressed weekly by a professor who was never available for office hours. His main contact with the university was the semiweekly section with a TA. In fact, when I began teaching at Staten Island Community College in 1972, I was surprised to discover that the City University of New York (CUNY) did not have such practices. My classes and those of my colleagues were relatively small. Today, things are different: My own CUNY graduate students now report they are entirely responsible for introductory sociology classes enrolling some eighty students at the Queens College and Hunter campuses of CUNY. At both campuses they receive no official—or, for that matter, unofficial—guidance, since the faculty is busy dealing with its own work overload.

So, the formation of the TAA at the University of Wisconsin (UW) prefigured a growing feeling of unease and even anger shared by many graduate students, then and now, a feeling that the encroaching multiversity concept—according to which only the research professor deserves the time to perform the work of knowledge production—had reached graduate education. From the perspective of the UW administration, graduate students were ready sources of teaching labor. But UW provided fertile ground for a militant response. As veterans of a mass antiwar struggle and of the southern civil rights summer projects, many students at UW had become near-professional organizers; they had experienced dealing with the administration and, perhaps equally important, knew how to deal with press and television. Moreover, the union idea was not foreign to these students, many of whom were influenced by Marxism or the radicalism of C. Wright Mills and local luminaries such as labor sociologist Maurice Zeitlin and especially William Appleman Williams, the great figure of burgeoning American revisionist history.

My advice was incidental to the course of events. After a strike, the administration recognized the TAA, negotiated a union contract, and promptly started a campaign to decertify it as bargaining agent. Briefly defeated, the TAA came back. For many of the same reasons that prompted the pioneer TA battle for unionization at UW, in the 1970s and 1980s TA unions emerged at the University of Michigan, at the University of California–Berkeley, and, in the 1990s, at Iowa and—most famously—Yale.

Since 1970, academic unionism has been far more successful among faculty, especially at the community college and state university levels. While there are some faculty unions in private colleges and universities, further unionization has been stymied by the U.S. Supreme Court's *Yeshiva* decision declaring faculty in private colleges and universities may not enjoy the protection of the labor relations law because the court considers them to be "management." The AFT is a large faculty union, but the American Association of University Professors (AAUP) and the National Education Association (NEA) have organized thousands of college teachers, some, like AFT, in major universities.

In fact, during the dismal 1980s, when, for the first time since the early years of the Depression, unions as a whole recorded a net loss of membership, faculty and academic unionism became one of the few growth fields in the labor movement. Before discussing the problems and possibilities of academic unionism, I want to address the context within which it has developed: the American university and its post–World War II transformations.

I

It is by now a commonplace that far from being a community of scholars dedicated to disinterested inquiry and intense intellectual dialogue, contemporary institutions of higher education are knowledge factories, substantial employers in many towns and cities that contribute significantly to the local economy, and, perhaps most of all, aging vats for a considerable fraction of the labor force. Needless to say, universities and colleges are by no means identical in their functions. Since the vast expansion of colleges and universities after World War II, higher-education institutions have arranged themselves along a loose, hierarchically constructed grid.

At the top are two tiers of research universities, which are dedicated to the production of knowledge for the socioeconomic system. Their products are destined for use in economic and social domains, chiefly corporations and the state—especially, but not exclusively, the military. The third tier consists of nearly all liberal arts and technical colleges. Whether intended to train elite or plebeian students, these colleges transmit the knowledge produced in research universities and, conventionally, have a major responsibility in the elite schools to impart the Western intellectual and moral tradition to students.

Since the 1960s, when the welfare state embarked upon its brief period of dramatic growth, and consumer society reached its maturity, women have massively entered the labor force, notably the professions. Spurred by feminism as much as by economic incentives since 1970, most female graduates of small, four-year private colleges and a relatively large proportion of state school graduates enter professional programs—in law and medical schools but also in institutions that prepare them for postsecondary teaching, social and private services, and research. The technical colleges, once the preferred site for producing middle-level computer specialists, are engaged preeminently in *training* students to take their (diminishing) places as computer programmers and technologists in the medical, engineering, chemical, biotechnology, and other industries.

The fourth tier includes the community colleges and two-year technical schools; their main job is to provide technicians to business and industry. A declining group of students use these schools as a stepping-stone to four-year programs, and in recent years the two-year degree has increasingly become terminal for the majority of community college students. And, given the shrinking demand for technical workers of all kinds, the community college is increasingly important as an *ideological* institution insofar as it fulfills, but only in the bureaucratic sense, the promise of higher education for all (Brint and Karabel 1989; Aronowitz and DiFazio 1994, ch. 8).

Since World War II, universities have mobilized—nearly monopolized—the preponderance of natural- and social-scientific knowledge production in proportion as knowledge has become the key productive force (Kenney 1986, 199). While major corporations retain considerable scientific and technical staffs who produce *practical* applications of theoretical and applied sciences, the responsibility for generating "new" knowledge is, despite draconian cuts in research budgets, still the domain of leading research universities. In effect, the state socializes the costs of research intended for use in privately held production and services through contracts let by the Pentagon, National Science Foundation, and the National Institutes of Health to "private" as well as public universities. The federal Departments of Agriculture, Labor, Commerce, Interior, Transportation, and Justice remain important sources of research funds, despite Congress's recent cost-cutting binge.

Before the 1980s, much of this knowledge had little or no immediate use; in effect, the largest government contractor, the Pentagon, subsidized much basic research because national science policy recognized the importance of *failure* as a vital ingredient of eventual success. But the tendency was to punish the failures that inevitably accompany theoretical and experimental reflection. Congress and the Clinton administration required that government grants be more dedicated, that is, be earmarked for practical, especially commodity, applications. This policy tended to discourage pure or useless research. America's leading magazine of the natural-science profession, *Science,* chronicles on a weekly basis both the reconfiguration of research toward industrial uses and the fears of scientists that, because of the precipitous decline of funding, the scientific enterprise is itself in jeopardy. In view of the enormous role that expensive machine technology plays in everyday research in physics and biology, the virtual end of funding for nondedicated work, especially theory, threatens to cripple U.S. science.

For example, funds are rapidly drying up for research not only in theoretical physics, especially in high-energy particle physics, but also in astronomy, cosmology, and other more esoteric endeavors. To be sure, solid-state physics has a ready source of research money in communications and information corporations. And the *vast* majority of funds for biological studies are devoted to producing new organisms for bioengineering. In this respect, private pharmaceutical corporations have entered into patent arrangements with relevant academic departments; in return for patent ownership, the corporations have donated substantial sums to the departments to offset losses of government funds.

II

Of the many "revolutions" of the post–World War II era—the dominance of technoscience over most aspects of everyday life, the second coming of consumer society, in many ways closely linked to technoscience's emergence—the veritable explosion of enrollments, of new colleges and universities, and of faculty in higher education may be the most important cultural event. While there can be no doubt that higher education has become a major industry in most regions of the country, it has also been one of the salient features of the doctrine according to which individuals may transcend the conditions of their birth, a hallmark of American ideology.

The aspiration for class mobility and the widespread faith that through credentials and hard work anyone can "make it" to a relatively lucrative career define our culture; and the doctrine that we make and remake ourselves through schooling has played an important part in discouraging collective action and expressions of social solidarity in favor of individual achievement. "Going to college" has become since the 1960s perhaps the main repository of the hopes and dreams of working-class blacks and Latinos for a brighter future for themselves and their children; some women have gone to college to avoid the trap of domesticity while others— in a historical moment of single parenthood—have seen a postsecondary degree as representing some expectation that they can find a job to support their families; and a growing proportion of white, working-class males who have suffered the incredible disappearance of good working-class jobs due to globalization, technological change, and the decline of the crafts have looked (reluctantly) to higher education to constitute the economic equivalent of what was once provided by the unionized workplace.

To a large extent, the claim that class origin was, in advanced industrial society, no longer destiny for those who kept their noses to the educational grindstone was richly fulfilled by the circumstances of the postwar era. The United States dominated the global economy for the quarter-century that ended about 1970. Its liberal credit system spurred production of a cornucopia of consumer goods available to anyone able to qualify for some deferred payment plan, and most of those goods were produced in the United States. And, as we have seen, from modest beginnings in the New Deal, the main features of the welfare state—mass education, Social Security, unemployment insurance, medical care for the aged and the poor, and federal housing subsidies for the "working middle class" as well as the poor—became a stabilizing force in our social and cultural system, legitimating the permanent war economy as well as persistent inequalities in wealth and income. After all, who cares about the rich getting richer as long as a substantial fraction of everybody else is getting theirs?

Faced with the return of eleven million members of the armed forces—about a sixth of the labor force—and an uncertain transition from wartime to peacetime economy, Congress enacted one of the most far-reaching measures in the history of welfare capitalism, the Servicemen's Readjustment Act (the GI Bill of Rights), which gave returning veterans free medical care, housing subsidies, and the right to return to school. About three million veterans availed themselves of their newly won educational opportunity, completing high school and filling a large number of seats in college classrooms. In 1945, private colleges and universities were more numerous than the relatively undeveloped public sector. Some states such as New York, California, and the major midwestern states had small public systems. The infusion of vast sums into higher education spurred an unprecedented building program in colleges and universities that, together with the postwar housing and auto boom, provided millions of jobs for construction and manufacturing workers.

By 1990, the number of colleges and universities had grown from about eighteen hundred in 1947 to thirty-two hundred, and student enrollments had increased from 2.3 million to 12.5 million (Lucas 1994). The beginnings of budget austerity in higher education in the early 1970s failed to deter the steady stream of students to higher education. In 1947, only 10 percent of high school graduates entered college; in 1960, 40 percent were accepted into two- and four-year colleges; by 1980, half of all graduates went on to higher education. Today, the number stands at 62 percent. Since 80 percent of those entering high school graduate, almost half of all youth enter college (Lucas 1994).

One of the less-noticed functions of U.S. and Canadian universities in the postwar period, during which the size of the young adult labor force has chronically outpaced job creation, is the degree to which they keep a considerable fraction of the labor force off the market. In 1994, 14.2 million students were enrolled in U.S. universities and colleges (the equivalent of 9 million full-time students). While many of these students are full- or part-time workers as well, it may be assumed that more than half of them would seek full-time employment if they were not in school. The United States leads all advanced industrial countries in postsecondary enrollments. Of about 150 million adults under age sixty-five, more than 9 percent attend some kind of higher-education program. In contrast, no European country enrolls more than 3 percent of its adults in these institutions, and most hover around 2 percent. In the 1960s, the British Higher Education Reform program began to emulate the U.S. model of high university enrollments, and France followed suit, largely after the May 1968 student-led revolt.

American universities are much more than training grounds for qualified or intellectual labor. They are aging vats for a considerable proportion of the labor force that would be otherwise unemployed. In many regions of the country, they are the major employer and the source of community income; even in some large cities such as New York and Chicago, colleges and universities are significant factors in the local and regional economies. And, culturally, universities embody the hopes, the aspirations, even the dreams of millions for a better future. Their fate is tied to the promise that here no rigid class system will stand in the way of substantial economic and social gain.

In Britain, Germany, and the United States, the New Left began, among other things, as a movement for university reform. In the United States, alongside the outpouring of students to participate in the southern civil rights movement and community organizing among the white and black poor in some northern cities, the question of what the university should be dominated the early years of the student movement. In Berkeley, the free speech movement emerged out of student protests against the House Un-American Activities Committee's foray into the Bay Area and the discontent with the perspective of the great theorist of the corporate university, UC-Berkeley chancellor Clark Kerr. According to Kerr, higher education is best defined in modern America in terms of the word "multiversity." In his report to the California governor and the legislature, Kerr generated a taxonomy according to which a legitimated three-tier system would prevail: at the pinnacle the research university, where professors would be, as much as possible, unburdened with heavy teaching loads in order to carry on the work of knowledge production; in the second tier, a panoply of four- and six-year institutions that would transmit knowledge to a technically credentialed student body; and, finally, a system of community colleges to provide *training* for lower-level technicians (Kerr 1972).

This system was to be geared to the segmented market for intellectual labor that emerged after the war with the establishment of a permanent war economy, the growing role of scientific knowledge in the form of computer and other automation processes in goods production, and the explosion of the tertiary (service) sector. Retail and wholesale services expanded rapidly; with the maturation of the welfare state, employment in state and local governments more than quadrupled and, by 1970, accounted for one of six jobs in the labor market. Many newly created professional, managerial, and administrative jobs required postsecondary credentials. Under these conditions, the academic system of American society became an important industry. In addition to its ideological role as purveyor and disseminator of "American" values and its task of *training* for the new knowledge-based industrial and service economy, it became a leading producer of knowledge. Kerr's program for a three-tier university system was oriented to these new tasks.

Kerr was brilliantly clear: Any intellectual culture would be concentrated at the top; the other tiers were to represent the requirement of the economy for new strata of professional and technical *personnel*. But, for Kerr and his colleagues in this emerging corporate culture, the *main task* of the university was to become a knowledge factory; its scientific culture was to be directed toward the means and the ends of economic growth and of public policy. The university was to become an instrument of state policy. Of course, there would be room for artistic and intellectual culture, but not everywhere. The main task of the public four-year and community colleges was to transmit technical knowledge to the second- and third-tier employees required by the labor market.

In the interest of this technocratic program for higher education, the UC-Berkeley administration declared students were barred from conducting political activity in behalf of "outside" interests on campus. This edict was directed at the civil rights movement as much as at radical parties and groups. But, when combined with Kerr's highly publicized multiversity taxonomy, the free speech movement's purview, which began with issues of political speech, rapidly extended to a critique of the corporate university and addressed itself to the poverty of student life in the age of the knowledge factory as well. At Michigan, Harvard, and many other leading campuses, students demanded a voice in the "decisions that affected their lives" and, in the words of Jerry Farber, likened the position of students to that of the "nigger."

Far from a self-perception, fostered by administration and by the media, of the elite universities as places of truly "higher" learning, many students increasingly saw themselves as powerless objects of the knowledge machine. Some eagerly devoured the writings of Paul Goodman, C. Wright Mills, Herbert Marcuse, and even Thorstein Veblen, whose *Higher Learning in America* (1918) could have been published today. Each had argued that the whole idea of education as a force for cultural renewal had been subverted by the mobilization of higher learning for instrumental ends, chiefly for the strengthening of increasingly concentrated economic, political, and cultural power (Goodman 1959; Marcuse 1964; Mills 1956).

The movement for student participation in all aspects of university governance, which entailed representation in key decision-making bodies as well as speech rights for "outside" organizations and individual dissenters, shook American universities precisely at the moment when the notion of students as a *market* or as *consumers* began to dominate administrative thinking. Consistent with the growing view of higher education as an industry, the older notion that colleges and universities were essentially decommodified institutions gave way to one in which what the universities produced was for sale. Thus, before World War II, universities were already accepting defense contracts to produce science and technology, a practice that sustained much of the research agendas of American universities for the next half-century. Under pressure caused by reduced government funding, some universities negotiated agreements with private corporations to cede the rights over bioengineering and solid-state physics "products" in return for sustained funding for research. In the context of the galloping commodification of scientific knowledge, the student as market became a logical next step.

Neoclassical economics construes consumer choice as the foundation of economic power. When a product fails in the market, it must be replaced. Thus, ultimate sovereignty in the market belongs to the consumer. On this model, universities must maintain high quality in order to attract students to buy their services. But how to measure the quality of educational services? In econometric models, Harvard, Yale, and other Ivy League schools are the best because they have a surfeit of student applicants who are willing to pay a premium price for their product. Accordingly, if the quality of the *credential*, measured in the number of jobs and the salaries offered to graduates by employers, declines, the consumer would cease to come. *That,* and not principally the various standards of academic evaluation, becomes the crucial criterion of the worth and standing of a university.

To the traditional academic mind, this account may seem somewhat crude. But the crudeness is the result of the selling of American universities as sources of cultural capital, which, as Pierre Bourdieu has correctly noted, is literally analogous to money capital. As universities have blatantly marketed themselves to business as knowledge- and human-capital producers and to students as cultural-capital providers, hardly anybody but the most devoted supplicant of the idea of the university as an independent community of scholars can doubt that the academic system corresponds more to the above description than to any other.

By the early 1960s, the new model was fairly well developed. The major problem remained the faculty. Except for some branches of the natural and social sciences that were well aware of the degree to which research had become subordinated to practical ends, most of the liberal arts faculty remained committed to the precepts of the older model and, for at least two decades, fought a rearguard battle to preserve the humanistic disciplines against encroachments such as administration efforts to transform English and philosophy in all but a few schools into service departments for largely technicized curriculum. The humanities as concept survive only in the first tier of elite universities comprising, in addition to the Ivy League schools, some small, private, four-year liberal arts colleges; the University of Chicago, Duke, Emory, and a few other private institutions; along with some of the leading state universities, especially the UC system, some Big Ten schools, and selected campuses of the New York State and City University systems.

But it was in these places that the students mounted their attack on the complicity of the universities with the military and corporations. It was in these elite universities that students faced the hostility of a liberal arts faculty still committed to an academic community that, even if it was not entirely dismantled, had already suffered considerably from the practical effects of the Kerr doctrine. At Berkeley, faculty opposition emanated from former socialists and communists such as sociologist Seymour Martin Lipset, for whom student protest was an invitation to the Right to intervene and was, for this reason, more dangerous to academic freedom than merely irresponsible. Like his colleague Lewis Feuer, a philosopher who saw in the student movement a *generational* revolt directed not only at liberal authority but at the Oedipal figure of the Father, Lipset discerned a definite authoritarian strain in the shrill demand for democratizing the campus. Steeped in Cold War fears, much of the liberal professoriat was skeptical of the incipient doctrine of participatory democracy within the universities. Already buffeted by new winds emanating from on high that they were not yet fully prepared to acknowledge, let alone accept, they were surely inhospitable to the idea of student academic citizenship (Feuer 1969).

Clearly, Lipset and Feuer understood student life neither as part of the emerging consumerist and corporatist culture (an analysis they ascribed to paranoia) nor as a democratic public sphere. The community of scholars, however diminished, needed defending—not against creeping commercialism but against the callow mob of violent, deformed, radicalized, middle-class brats. The free speech movement succeeded not only in winning the right to engage in political activity but also, in many places around the country, in securing a measure of academic citizenship. Token student representatives were elected to boards of trustees and, in the departments, to various committees. Needless to say, faculty were not pleased, but the strength of the movement imposed, putatively, a new regime upon them, as administrations hastened to accommodate to the new political reality that students, through protest and press visibility, constituted, for a time, a new power on campus, one that reappeared in the 1980s under the sign of political correctness.

Yet, despite its reservations, the liberal arts faculty became some of the chief beneficiaries of the university reform movement. Conservative to the core, dormant faculty senates and councils bestirred themselves to debate the future of the university, organized unions, formed women's and black and Latino studies programs and departments, and, under the impetus of the radicalized student movement, engaged in educational innovation manifested most visibly in the development of ethnic, women's, American, and cultural studies on many campuses.

Seen in this context, the fiscal crisis of public education became an occasion for the recentralization of universities and may, perhaps unintentionally, mark the end of the brief period of academic innovation begun by junior faculty, especially women and African Americans, in the 1970s. Thirty years after the emergence of student power, as we reach the end of the New Deal, Fair Deal, and Great Society era in which public goods enjoyed a position of some privilege, governmentality is itself in question. In the 1990s, under a centrist Democratic national administration and equally conservative local governments, the state's repressive functions overpower and mediate its diminishing social functions. For the Clinton administration, defending a provision of the welfare state could be undertaken only on condition that it be combined with a new manifestation of social conservatism. Police now routinely patrol public schools and universities as if they were identical with the mean streets of the central cities. The concern with educational parsimony in the face of legislative budget cutting eclipses the concern with democratization that accompanied the rise of the black freedom and women's movements in the late 1960s.

III

Since the late 1980s, the academic system of American society has undergone another process of profound transformation. But the logic was already established during the "golden age" of the immediate post–World War II era. Having adopted the framework and the ideology of the large corporation, universities and colleges—private as well as public—are "downsizing" in the name of rising costs compared to declining or stagnant revenues, but they also have used budget cuts to effect a decisive power shift from faculty to administration. In multicampus universities such New York's state and City University systems, the California state university system, and many others, the slogan "academic planning" has been used to remove authority over curricular decisions from the local campus community to the central administration. As the institutions have become more bureaucratized in the past twenty years, presidents and chancellors resemble CEOs rather than academic leaders. Their central functions are fund-raising, lobbying, and diplomacy, which, increasingly, are the same thing. For the most part, their grasp of the mission of the university has been articulated in terms of (a) the job market and (b) the stock market. The intellectual mission of the academic system now exists as *ornament*, that is, as a legitimating mechanism for a host of other functions, primarily the production and transmission of useful knowledge.

   The priority of knowledge as *instrument* over *substance* places scholars and critics in an ambiguous position. Unless their writing and teaching can be situated within the corporate university's ongoing functions, except for the most prominent consensus intellectuals among them, they are regarded by funders and administrators as redundant except as purveyors of "critical thinking" in the elite undergraduate curriculum. There they enjoy a relatively comfortable existence, but one that is progressively marginal and anxiety-ridden precisely because the self-perception of the humanities is that they have lost considerable status in the newly restructured academic system.

Both in their methods and in their self-understanding of their role, the social sciences in this system have modeled themselves on the natural sciences. Theory no longer has a guiding role in the disciplines; it is relegated to a not very important subdiscipline. The crucial branches are those having to do with policy, those that can be considered state social science. In sociology, criminology has once more emerged as the leading field; those interested in academic and research jobs are advised to build a sufficient claim to this field. This transformation is entirely complete in economics and political science, is hegemonic in sociology but still contested, and has not (yet) dominated anthropology, which, in any case, may prove moot because of the crisis created by the loss of (Third World) domain in the postcolonial age.

Public universities—most typically the State University of New York (SUNY), the City University of New York (CUNY), and the California State University (CSU)—have received a clear signal from their respective governors and state legislatures either that the moment of mass public higher education is over or, if it is not technically ended, that the faculty must reconcile itself to becoming managers of ever-larger classes typical of Kerr's vision of the multiversity. In a recent decision of its board of trustees—a body of outside appointees, consisting mostly of corporate executives, lawyers, ex-politicians, and "civic" leaders recruited from the philanthropic upper crust and the black and Latino middle class—CUNY has sharply curtailed its open admissions policy by, among other "reforms," reducing to one year its commitment to provide so-called remedial courses for academically unprepared students, many of whom are immigrants requiring language training before or concurrent with entering the ordinary academic curriculum. "What the City University and other public systems have done," according to *New York Times* reporter Joseph Berger, "is to shift remediation from four year colleges to two year community colleges. The community colleges are cheaper places for remedial courses because professors are required to teach more hours, classes are larger, and in New York, a greater proportion of tuition payments can be used to pay for remedial classes" (*New York Times*, June 27, 1995).

In sum, the university's restructuring means that community colleges have been designated as the solution for a broad range of students requiring an extra boost on the way to credentials. The only problem is that the process has been designed on the basis of the celebrated Joseph Heller narrative: "We want to help you, but we will set impossible conditions for our helpers." Like the roach motel, students can still get in, but they can't get out except as intellectual corpses.

But, following the trend of the private corporate sector, where literally tens of thousands of professional and technical employees have been shed since the stock market crash of 1987, state and local governments, suffering declining tax revenues because of sinking real income, have followed suit by cutting their own workforces. And, in step with the steady march of Congress to dismantle key elements of the welfare state, especially federal aid to education, health care, and social services, the proprietors of state governments have begun to argue that if there are fewer jobs in these service delivery systems, as well as in banks and insurance companies whose clerical and professional workforces are increasingly subject to mergers and acquisitions and technological displacement, then maintaining expanded professional and technical education will only flood the market with credentialed, but unneeded, workers. Hence, the drive to raise admission standards in order to restrict enrollments to academically qualified students. The new public university systems' slogan might be, "Give me your qualified and deserving poor."

These broad changes are already taking their toll on graduate programs. Facing draconian cuts in student aid, many programs limit the number of students they admit to only those who can be supported by the money available. Since many schools are raising teacher workloads, and faculty are required to teach more undergraduate, particularly lower-division, courses, many have no time to teach graduate courses. As the number of graduate courses declines, seminars turn into lecture courses, and lecture courses become experiments in mass postgraduate education. The core of traditional graduate education, the one-to-one relation between mentor and mentee, is eroding as graduate school more resembles undergraduate college.

IV

The idea of the university has, like much of our moral and intellectual culture, religious roots. In medieval and Renaissance Europe, the *collegium* was formed first in the monastery or, among Jews, in the "school" as a community of scholars who together studied the sacred texts and wrote commentaries on them. Their readings became the basis of religious teaching to the underlying population. In this regime, the college was *primarily* constituted as a space for the search for knowledge of God, but it also evolved into more secular areas such as science and art.

The early "secular" colleges were similarly constituted. They remained church-sponsored, and church officials assumed the task of maintaining the institution—primarily its buildings and finance. But faculty retained authority over the curriculum and pedagogy. That did not eliminate conflicts between the two governance structures of the college, but lines of authority were far more clearly delineated than now.

Nowadays, our concept of academic freedom in the university is one-dimensional. We understand and generally support the right of individual faculty members to speak and write according to the dictates of their own consciences and remain free of legal or administrative sanction. It has become an aspect of speech protected by the spirit and the letter of the First Amendment. The many violations of this meaning of academic freedom, especially denial of tenure to the unconventional and dismissal and administrative intimidation of dissenters, have been vigorously opposed by the aggrieved, by professional associations, by faculty unions, and by civil liberties organizations.

We associate the institution of tenure with the need to protect dissenting faculty from sanction imposed by the public, the administration of the university, and colleagues who might be prone to punish apostates. Before World War II, however, tenure was rarely awarded to the garden-variety instructor. No less a figure than critic Lionel Trilling held the rank of an untenured instructor at Columbia throughout the 1930s; in 1936 he almost lost his English department job because he was a Marxist, held Freudian beliefs, and was a Jew; he achieved real job security only after the war. In fact, as a practice, tenure is barely a half-century old. In 1940 the AAUP issued a statement saying that the only way to secure academic freedom was through tenure, and tenure was gradually instituted by most universities after World War II.

But the AAUP's widely discussed 1940 proposal, which had first been enunciated in 1915, is once again under attack (Lucas 1994, 197–200). The president of the University of Minnesota recently floated a proposal to abolish tenure; the president of Bennington College actually got rid of it along with a number of tenured faculty; and prominent colleges such as the New School, Eugene Lang, and Hampshire, among many others, do not offer anything more than multiyear contracts.

Further, the second dimension of academic freedom, the rights of the faculty as a *collectivity* to retain sovereignty over the educational process, has been buried with the restructuring. Questions such as whether a department or program should be established, expanded, retained, or eliminated; hiring and dismissal of faculty; assignment of positions to programs and departments; workloads and classroom sizes—these arc only a few of the crucial decisions affecting schools that have gradually been assumed by administrations and by boards of trustees.

In the midst of these changes, nearly all higher-education institutions have maintained the formal apparatus of faculty sovereignty and have made only tentative gestures, so far, toward challenging institutions such as tenure and faculty-based academic review. Promotion and tenure committees still deliberate on individual cases; faculty-administration retrenchment committees decide on how to reduce staff in times of budget crisis (within parameters established by the administration and, where applicable, the union contract); curriculum committees continue to approve or refuse new courses or programs; and student affairs committees, now reduced to an aspect of the policing function of administration, monitor and make disciplinary decisions on academic and extra-academic student performance.

But in both the public and the private university sectors, power has slowly but surely shifted to administrators, who retain final determination of nearly all university issues. Faculty senates and academic committees are really advisory bodies whose recommendations are no longer routinely approved by higher authorities. Everywhere, departmental and divisional recommendations for tenure (or its refusal) are subject to reversal by deans and presidents. And curriculum issues are now subordinated to budget considerations.

It should be evident to all but the most myopic observer that the worst abuses of the *collegium* have been in the abrogation of faculty sovereignty by the corporate university, even as cases of individual academic-freedom violations are the most visible. The disparity between reality and public awareness may not be ascribed to conspiracy or entirely to evil intent. The centralization of the academic system is a product of what Alan Trachtenberg has called "the incorporation of America" (Trachtenberg 1988). Just as the family-owned firm and the craft union or guild have been relegated to a subordinate existence in the U.S. political economy, so the *collegium* occupies a purgatory between the heaven of the corporate university boardroom and the hell of the huge lecture halls that dominate public universities. It has a voice with little authority; its crafts—reading, writing, speaking—suffer a wizened existence; its minions, embattled and dispirited, have mounted resistance in the last five years, but these efforts are sporadic, disorganized, and only partially effective.

Thus, we can see the steamroller at work. For example, during the last budget crisis, many CUNY presidents and the chancellor's office exempted professional administrators from the retrenchment plan and planted the burden of the layoffs or thinly disguised force-outs on low-level administrative and clerical staff. The corporate culture was firmly in place. At many public universities in the past two decades, faculty hiring was virtually frozen at most campuses while, at the same time, administrative hiring experienced a veritable boom. This fact is a measure of the power shift during this period. The question that must be addressed is why and how the faculty lost its sovereignty. Before dealing with this issue, however, one other question must be discussed: Does the *collegium* include students? Is the power shift a violation of their academic freedom?

Symptomatically, we now speak of a corporate "culture," which in the academy signifies a *displacement* of the old intellectual culture of the sciences, humanities, and the arts. Research and writing go on, but they become increasingly instrumental to the overarching goals of individual survival (or, in some cases, to advancement in the academic hierarchy) and, more to the point, a means to enhance the coffers and, secondarily, the prestige of the institution. The individual who pursues knowledge for its own sake or for human betterment may still perform this work on her/his own time. In contrast, faculty are, more than ever, urged, cajoled, and even threatened to direct their scholarship and research to the ever-decreasing pots of grants gold on penalty of losing promotions, tenure, and resources such as computer time, assistants, and equipment.

In the process, it is no wonder faculty feel like employees rather than a series of communities devoted to common intellectual concerns. In consideration of their new, proletarianized status, many have joined unions and converted their faculty senates into bodies that are adversarial to administration and legislatures that, in their perception, are bosses just like any other. Increasingly, the institutions of faculty control are losing their status and, from the perspective of administration, are, at best, viewed as a nuisance whose utility for purposes of legitimation may have (over)reached its limit. While faculty, including adjuncts and teaching assistants, have reevaluated their traditional antipathy to collective action as a means to adjudicate their grievances, they view unions as the unions see themselves—that is, as economic bargaining agents concerned chiefly with salaries, workload, and job security issues.

Today, approximately one-quarter of full-time faculty and non-supervisory administrative staff are organized in three unions: the AFT, with about eighty-five thousand members; the AAUP, with about twenty-two thousand members under contract, although its total membership is about forty-four thousand; and the NEA, with about 100,000 members. The unions bargain for faculty at some leading universities: The AAUP has organized Rutgers and Wayne State and has dual affiliation at CUNY with AFT and at Cal State, the nation's largest public college system, with NEA, the primary bargaining agency. The AFT is the primary union at SUNY, where its affiliate has twenty-two thousand in the bargaining unit, the largest academic union in the country; at CUNY, with about thirteen thousand; and at Temple and the Pennsylvania State University system of former teachers' colleges (not Penn State); and at Illinois and California community colleges. The union has won collective bargaining at the University of California (U Cal) for teaching assistants and lab workers, but not for faculty, although it has locals in most of the U Cal campuses. Some private colleges and universities, notably Long Island (AFT) and Saint John's (AAUP), are unionized. TAs are affiliated with unions ranging from the AFT to the United Electrical, Radio, and Machine Workers of America (Iowa) and the Hotel Employees and Restaurant Employees International Union (Yale). Clerical and maintenance workers in universities are organized into many unions, notably the American Federation of State, County, and Municipal Employees, the United Auto Workers (UAW), and the Service Employees International Union.

These employees are not included in the exemption provided by the notorious *Yeshiva* decision, and so clerical and maintenance unions have made significant inroads in private universities such as Harvard, Columbia, Yale, and Boston University. Their strength is characteristically concentrated in the Northeast, still the largest bastion of unionism in services.

Apart from the private colleges, which faculty unions believe are, for the time being, outside the realm of possible unionization, the glaring weakness remains the public research universities where faculty enjoy considerably higher salaries than in the third- and fourth-tier institutions and where many faculty earn significant outside income as consultants. With their long-term job prospects ever more grim, TAs increasingly seek union organization. Apart from the exceptions already noted, faculty at research institutions such as U Cal, Texas, Penn State, Virginia, and the Big Ten universities generally view themselves as exempt from the imperative of collective action since they are convinced that their professional fate is, for all intents and purposes, a function of their individual talents and achievements. U Cal and many other public universities reward faculty according to merit, which is gained primarily by publishing articles in certain journals, publishing academically respectable books, and engaging in funded research.

Even when resources and pay have been cut by state legislatures, most of these faculty remain indifferent, if not antagonistic, to unionism because, I suspect, they fear to admit that their own position, in absolute terms, has deteriorated even if their relative status and working conditions are princely compared to colleagues at state and most private two- and four-year colleges. In fact, in proportion as public colleges and universities suffer vocationalization, faculty and staff reductions, and deteriorating working conditions, the cultural, as opposed to the economic, position of the elite university professoriat increases. Salary stagnation notwithstanding, the status gap between the various tiers of the academic system is widening.

Like teachers in the primary and secondary schools, professors organized unions when they understood that their diminished cultural capital would not sustain their economic and professional positions, especially in absolute terms; that regardless of the pedigree of their graduate and undergraduate degrees, they were being ground down by increasingly arbitrary administrations and vindictive legislatures, especially after the Vietnam War era; that as salaried employees they needed the advantages of collective action. More to point, they had to surrender, to a certain degree, professional illusions, especially the pernicious doctrine of genius and talent inherited from the nineteenth century.

Professors' first move as trade unionists was to frame their organizations in the images of conventional business or economistic unionism. Understandably, the more trade unionist the faculty, the more antiprofessional. Of course, although unions of professionals were never able to entirely avoid dealing with professional issues, their first responsibility was to assert, against the prevailing wisdom, that professors' interests were closer to those of the labor movement than to management. In this respect, CUNY is an example of an ideologically moderate leadership, which nonetheless steadfastly resisted the concept of merit as the basis of salary determinations. To be sure, promotions and tenure were and remain the last bastion of the merit system, but salary increases within academic rank are awarded on the basis of length of service. In contrast, many other union contracts retain management's right to distribute academic rewards subject only to the grievance procedure.

There is still much convincing to be done with perhaps a majority of the professoriat, in and out of the unions. Trained within professional ideology, most professors in research universities see themselves neither as intellectuals nor as teachers, which, in either case, would result in a politicizing reflexivity. Consequently, many union members share with other professors a primary identity with their professional associations and seek approval from colleagues within their discipline and, ultimately, from the university administration that retains the purse strings, rather than from the class of intellectuals to which they putatively belong.

The research university faculty may do better, but they are not doing particularly well. With diminished funds for research, many are teaching more than ever. Many have been forced to live primarily on their salaries, a change that, in some cases, reduced their incomes by as much as half. Austerity in research funding has been matched by legislative parsimony. Faculty salaries at leading universities have barely kept pace with inflation and are, absent a few thousand chair holders and academic stars (whose incomes nevertheless rarely exceed $150,000 a year), modest in comparison to medicine and corporate law, with which, by education at least, they are on par. Still, when they look down at their colleagues in nonresearch universities, where a full professor earns an average of $78,000 a year, somewhat in excess of $20,000 more than a beginning assistant professor, their $70,000 to $75,000 salaries look good if not sumptuous.

There can be little doubt of past union effectiveness in vastly improving faculty and staff salaries, working conditions, and benefits. Until recently, CUNY salaries compared favorably with nearly all major private and public universities and, for a time, were the highest, on average, in the country. But the fiscal crisis of 1975–1976 and parallel legislative cutbacks of funds for public universities in many states combined with faculty reticence to strike (except in some community colleges, the dramatic TA strike at Yale, and the faculty strike at Temple) and otherwise take direct action to win their demands are decisively shifting the balance between public and private universities. Faculty unions still make a difference, but, like unions in manufacturing and many services, recently their advantage may be that they provide a grievance procedure and a broad range of benefits rather than increases in salaries.

What is less clear is whether unions see themselves as agents in the wider university life. Until now, the fundamental power grab by university administrations has not elicited a strong response by campus unions. Some, like CUNY's Professional Staff Congress (PSC) and SUNY's United University Professions (UUP), have addressed issues of academic planning. UUP thwarted an administration proposal to privatize the two SUNY medical schools and medical centers; PSC played an important role in helping to remove several college presidents who were acting against the interests of faculty and students. The union recently joined in a successful suit against the CUNY board of trustees for its premature declaration of financial exigency before the state budget was completed, declaring that the action was a ploy to force retrenchments and most importantly organizational changes not warranted by the budget situation. Yet, beyond these and some other instances, faculty unions have seen themselves in a severely restricted compass; for understandable reasons they have made the sphere of economic bargaining, including job security, their special province. Issues such as the creation of new programs, the elimination of old departments, and major curricular changes are, in a rough division of labor, understood to be the province of the faculty senates and the administration.

PSC's active participation in the creation of City College's Center for Worker Education and its collaboration with a major literacy center in New York City, the Consortium for Worker Education, may be exceptions to the rule of noninvolvement in educational innovation. Yet if recent bipartisan assaults on higher education persist, faculty unions may be obliged to consider whether to become leading vehicles for counterplanning if faculty senates—which are frequently dominated by the most senior professors, who shuttle back and forth from faculty to administration—lack the political will to oppose downsizing/reorganization programs aimed at vocationalization.

V

What has been the response of faculty and students to the new regime of educational disaccumulation? Where there is an organized response, it has been confined to resistance. I want to offer CUNY's experience in the 1990s as a case study of what is possible and of what faculty and students have perceived to be the limits of their power. In spring 1995, faculty and student organizations, including PSC, effectively mobilized to oppose the new Republican governor's proposal to cut the university's budget by more than 15 percent and Mayor Rudolph Giuliani's threat to cut off $20 million from community colleges. Thousands demonstrated, called public meetings, and lobbied legislators on behalf of blocking the budget cuts. At the campus level, some faculty fought administration-sponsored "retrenchment plans" that proposed to eliminate entire departments and programs rather than anticipate across-the-board cuts. In the end, the cuts did result in some departmental closings and layoffs, but early expectations that some state campuses would be discontinued and the two state university medical centers would be privatized never became reality because of adroit efforts of the UUP and the state's teachers' federation, which led an intense legislative lobby.

Even as the coalition opposing the cuts celebrated its partial victory, the governor's budget proposals for SUNY and CUNY in 1996–1997 and beyond stepped up the pressure for reorganization and downsizing. While denouncing the proposed cuts, administrations at both universities used the occasion to begin a process of academic planning from above aimed at sharply reducing the liberal arts to service departments for enhanced professional and technical programs. Accelerating tendencies built into both systems, administration plans called for the overt establishment of a few research-oriented campuses while relegating most to vocational roles.

While resistance is necessary, it is hardly sufficient to address the systematic dismantling of the democratic mission of the university. On the whole, the educational imaginary of faculty and students has been limited to preserving the existing state of affairs—especially the much-maligned open admissions policy—rather than being devoted to generating ideas for a different kind of restructuring of the university that would not diminish access but would radically improve the curriculum, pedagogy, and school governance. Even the most progressive have hesitated to propose anything innovative or even different, fearing that any change could only enhance the administration's drive to further centralization.

Like so many other struggles in this corporate "downsizing" era, the Right has all the ideas and the opposition finds itself backed into a corner: The liberals have become the conservatives, the most staunch defenders of the status quo. For example, in the fight to prevent the dismantling of the archaic welfare system, the "Left" seems to have forgotten its own critique of the cynicism of the welfare bureaucracy; it has now become the most fervent defenders of a system it once excoriated. Similarly, whereas educational radicals (not to be confused with the traditional left liberals) once condemned the disciplinary basis of school knowledge as an outmoded, repressive regime, many now resist any hint of educational reform, since such proposals rarely signify the enlargement of resources but are used by administration to facilitate consolidation.

On the run, the liberals have steadfastly refused to enter a serious dialogue with their adversaries. For example, critics howled when CUNY Chancellor W. Anne Reynolds announced the College Preparatory Initiative (CPI) in 1993, a program that would force high schools to raise graduation standards by offering serious language, science, and math courses; the stated goal of the program was to relieve the university of some of the obligations of providing remedial programs, obligations that would then be taken care of by secondary school curricula. The critics simply refused to believe that CPI was more than a thinly veiled effort to phase out open admissions. Perhaps they were correct.

Yet who can deny urban high schools need significant reform? Those concerned with preserving open admissions might have explored the possibility of joining the chancellor in fighting to upgrade the curricula of many of New York's high schools. It would have entailed finding new money for laboratories, hiring math and language teachers, and, perhaps equally significant, reforming administrative structures in secondary education. Specifically, educational reformers in the schools have successfully argued that the factory-like, monolithic high schools containing two to four thousand students are inimical to learning. In New York City, some two dozen smaller schools, each enrolling about five hundred students, have been established in the last twenty years, most of them since the late 1980s. School districts have extended their alternative intermediate schools to high schools, introducing a 7–12 concept for secondary school. And the board of education has approved breaking up some existing big high schools that are not working into smaller houses. So far, the results have been encouraging, if inconclusive.

The higher-educational Democrats are, with exceptions, not part of this movement. Rather they are stuck in a sniping, marginal position, refusing to acknowledge that many New York high schools aren't working. Or, even if they agree that students come to CUNY and other large urban university systems without sufficient academic preparation, their deep suspicion of the administration's motives for undertaking reform produces a state of paralysis.

The paranoid style of politics is entirely understandable in this environment. Bereft of ideas, the university administration demands of the campuses "academic planning," which almost everyone knows is a euphemism for adapting to the new downsizing programs mandated by the bond holders, who are, at least symbolically, represented on the board of trustees. Still, we must ask whether it makes sense to deny everything and construct the fight entirely in terms of resistance.

In August 1993, the CUNY administration, at a moment when their plan for top-down academic planning had been almost universally rejected by faculty and students, asked me what would be an alternative. I suggested that a faculty-controlled committee award small grants to groups who would propose and attempt to implement domain-based, rather than disciplinary-based, curricula. Each proposal, I suggested, would have to involve faculty from different disciplines and even different campuses. Working with Dean Ronald Berkman of the chancellor's staff, we procured from the Aaron Diamond Foundation enough funds for awarding some fifteen grants over a three-year period.

As I developed the program, some faculty warned me of the risks: Working with the administration at a time of severe budget crisis would invite the perception that what we called "New Visions in Undergraduate Education" was simply a backdoor through which the "Goldstein Report," the main incarnation of the administration's own proposal, would sneak through. Neither participating faculty—those on the committee and the applicants—nor the administration understood "New Visions" to be other than what it purported to be: an alternative approach to academic planning. We were not being co-opted. We were aggressively intervening in the crisis, in this case not with protest but with affirmative alternatives.

Tacitly rejecting the either/or of protest and collaboration, members of the committee have protested the governor's and mayor's assault on the City University. We have, as individual faculty members, testified, lobbied legislators, and marched before City Hall. Some of us have given press and television interviews expressing complete opposition to the prevailing program to gut the institution. Yet we saw the virtue of entering the planning process; that a dialogue has not genuinely ensued is a function both of our own inability to broaden the approach in the context of the debate and of the way in which the discourse of crisis has hardened positions on both sides.

Needless to say, the great battle for higher education did not end when, in the face of massive protests, the legislature and the governor scaled back the cuts and the university's shortfall was closed by raising tuition by $750 for senior college students and $400 for community colleges. More than a dozen programs were shut down in 1995, and we can expect new stages in the crisis: Once again, facing reduced revenues (a reduction produced, fundamentally, by the legacy of bipartisan tax concessions to business and the wealthy, the governor's own tax cut, and the recession in the state's economy), the governor will try to radically reduce the budgets for public education—both the lower and higher institutions. Heaving a sigh of regret, the university administration will be forced by these new budgetary calumnies to consider closing several colleges, retrenching faculty, and closing thousands of courses. Once again, faculty and students will face the choice of protest or alternative.

A small but dedicated group has joined in sustaining the CUNY coalition that has consistently fought the budget cuts; some of these activists have formed a new caucus within the union to provide more determined and imaginative leadership to the faculty. And the groups working on new curricula have not surrendered hope; in some cases, their plans have been realized in new undergraduate programs. But the obstacles are formidable. Many are deeply committed to their own disciplines and to professional and technical education. They are willing to resist reductions that hurt their own programs but are unwilling to entertain new approaches that might entail radically rethinking their own professional status. Some, indeed, are in a state of deep denial. They hope for renewal on the basis of a new liberal state government, economic growth, or a surge of political support for public education (which, in spring 1996, seemed to have emerged somewhat). And a considerable portion of the most thoughtful and experienced faculty have already left for other universities or have retired rather than suffer the humiliation of standing on the deck of a sinking ship.

The deep issue is, of course, power. Have the faculty and student communities effectively surrendered the vision of the community of scholars and now accepted their already institutionalized status as employees and consumers? Or is there still hope that in addition to the rituals of resistance (which, it must be admitted, can slow the steamroller down but not stop it), these communities, recognizing they are in the same boat, will abandon the moralistic, ritualized, paranoid style for a more nuanced, and ultimately strategic, effort to fight for a democratic university? Although a democratic university would include some of the elements of the hard-won open admissions policy, it would go beyond it to ask the fundamental question: What is the mission of the university in a postwork society? Can we disengage the orientation to jobs, jobs, jobs and to a corporate culture to found our own?

The answers to these questions are ineluctably linked to other issues: What is political will? Who are the agents? What is the program? Beyond rage lurks a new approach. Whether we will stumble on it before we have been locked into antagonistic and ultimately futile positions remains to be seen.

For academic unions there can be no question of reversing the tendency toward the de facto end of mass public higher education through collective bargaining. Having successfully shown that the professoriat in some academic precincts can act like traditional trade unionists without seriously damaging their academic integrity or standing, the unions are now faced with the awesome task of becoming institutions of alternative as well as resistance. In short, they are challenged to accept responsibility for the academic system rather than remaining representatives of specific interests of faculty and staff within its technocratically defined boundaries. The challenge is to become agents of a new educational imagination—that is, to join with others in counterplanning that aims both to retain mass higher education as a right and to suggest what education is in the new, postregulation, postwork era.

◇

7

Should Academic Unions Get Involved in Governance?

The steady corporatization of American higher education has threatened to relegate faculty governance, never strong, to the historical archive. In the twentieth century, scholars—notably Thorstein Veblen, Robert S. Lynd, C. Wright Mills, and Richard Hofstadter—deplored the tendency for boards of trustees and high-level administrators to concentrate power in their own hands and for corporations and corporate foundations to play a more prominent role in governance of some institutions of higher learning. These dire warnings have largely come to pass, and the past quarter century has witnessed a powerful trend toward the disenfranchisement of faculty. The introduction of online degrees in public and private colleges and universities, the reshaping of curricula to meet particular corporate needs, the systematic starving of the liberal and fine arts amid the expansion of technical and business programs, and the increasing importance of competitive sports are just some of the elements of the vast transformation that has spared few institutions. Add to these the openly sanctioned comparison between college presidents and corporate CEOs and the unembarrassed justification of paying academic presidents high-six-figure salaries. Where are the forces that are prepared to defend true higher learning? Who will address the new challenges to academic autonomy posed by proposals for periodic tenure review, signs that some administrators are prepared to use political and ideological criteria in tenure cases, and the thorny question of who owns the intellectual property generated by faculty innovations? In short, how can we defend the fragile institutions of academic freedom?

131

The conventional answer is faculty senates and councils, of course. Didn't the Harvard faculty succeed in driving its sitting president from office? Haven't faculty assemblies and representative bodies voted "no confidence" in errant and arrogant administrators who, when the pressure has been unbearable, occasionally have chosen retirement or resignation rather than risking a costly and embarrassing struggle to keep their jobs? A close examination of these relatively rare instances of the exercise of faculty prerogatives through the senates' collective action would show that most of these cases occurred in research universities and elite private colleges. But of the more than 4,000 institutions of higher education, only about 300 fall into these categories. The rest are public colleges and universities controlled directly by state legislatures because the legislatures appropriate budgets and must approve the appointment of all top administrators; community colleges, which are often subsumed under county legislatures and sometimes are accountable to the state as well; and second- and third-tier private institutions, which in some parts of this country operate as fiefdoms subject to the will of their respective boards of trustees and presidents.

In these schools, academic freedom is sometimes a state devoutly to be wished. But the root of the problem of faculty governance in the overwhelming majority of schools is the institutional, quasi-juridical limits on the powers of faculty senates. At best they have a degree of moral authority stemming from endangered tradition. On the whole, faculty councils and senates are advisory bodies to the administration; they possess no formal institutional power and in many cases are controlled by administrators who sit on their executive bodies because of the fiction that they are faculty on leave to perform the necessary tasks of administration but intend to return to the ranks. The facts that members of senates and councils are elected and that these bodies appoint committees to review curricula, tenure, and promotion decisions barely disguise the reality that the president and her or his administration have final authority. Whereas this authority was once regarded as little more than a "rubber stamp" of decisions made by faculty, it is no longer uncommon for the president to overturn the decision of a professional and budget committee, sometimes on behalf of an aggrieved candidate but most often against departmental and campuswide committees that recommend tenure and promotion of the candidate or seek to implement program innovations.

Underlying these conflicts is that in the private academic sector, boards of trustees and top administrators have absolute control of the budget. But there is another factor influencing the decline of faculty governance: So-called executive pay plans set middle and top administrators' pay and perks at levels significantly above those of faculty, creating an unbridgeable gulf between faculty and administration. Although it is still true that most institutions recruit their top and middle administrators from the ranks of faculty, once in positions such as dean, provost, and president, few return to the ranks of the professoriate after their terms of office. Instead, when an administrator's term is over, he or she may enter the private sector executive job market and trust for the future to headhunting firms. Administration becomes for most, if not all, a career that brings with it substantial financial rewards compared to faculty salaries. Broadly speaking, it may be argued that, in keeping with the corporate nature of the institution, academic administrators have become a part of the professional and managerial class.

Although it is still convenient to pay lip service to what is now termed "shared governance," since the boundary between faculty and administration has continued to harden, it is no longer in administrators' interest to empower faculty. In public institutions, faculty disempowerment has been codified by law; legislatures, the governor or county executive, and their staffs or state boards of higher education reserve all rights except those that have been wrested by academic unions, which, alone in the academic community, still possess formal if not substantive autonomy. The relative powerlessness of most faculty senates and the independence of unions suggest the possibility that the long-term trend toward faculty disempowerment may be reversed if unions choose to become involved in governance on behalf of their members. It is a long shot for a number of reasons, not least of which is that private sector faculty remains largely outside unions.

A little-known fact: Since the 1970s, academic unions have been among the few sectors of the labor movement that have experienced significant growth. As large sections of unionized manufacturing workplaces disappeared, academic labor began to stir and to unionize. In the past thirty-five years, the three major academic unions—the National Education Association (NEA), the American Federation of Teachers (AFT), and the American Association of University Professors (AAUP)—have added more than 200,000 members among the professoriate, and thousands of university and college professional, clerical, and maintenance employees have won union representation as well. Today, in terms of density—the proportion of union members to the labor force—academic labor is among the highest represented in the union movement. A third of the total nonmanagerial academic labor force is represented by unions—most, but not all, in public institutions. Missing from the unionized are professors in most of the leading private and public research universities and in private four-year liberal arts colleges, although clerical, professional, and graduate-student employees have significant union density in these institutions.

Prior to the 1980 Supreme Court ruling in the fateful so-called *Yeshiva* decision (*National Labor Relations Board v. Yeshiva University,* 444 U.S. 672) that college professors in private institutions are managers because they participate in the governance of the university or college and are thus ineligible for protection under the Labor Relations Act, union growth in the private academic sector was quite healthy. In the 1960s and 1970s, faculty at Long Island University, St. John's, Hofstra, Adelphi, and other large universities won union recognition and continue to maintain their contracts. Until 2005, the National Labor Relations Board (NLRB) ruled that graduate assistants at private institutions of higher education were not managers and that in research and teaching tasks they were employees, not students. Graduate assistants at Columbia, University of Pennsylvania, Brown, Yale, and New York University (NYU) joined thousands of graduate-student employees in leading public universities such as the Universities of California and Michigan to secure union organization. Except for NYU, which initially recognized and bargained with the union, the university administrations have declined to recognize the graduate-assistant unions and have successfully resisted several strikes. But graduate-teaching and research-assistant unionization suffered a blow in 2005 when the Labor Relations Board ruled that these people were students and not employees, even though they taught a sizable portion of the undergraduate courses and were paid. In 2005–2006, NYU graduate assistants conducted a losing strike when the administration took advantage of the board ruling and refused to recognize the union unless it forfeited most of the assistants' rights.

During the period of growth and consolidation, academic unionism faced a series of constraints dictated by state law and by the unions' acceptance of traditional trade-union culture. During the struggles for union recognition, academic employees were obliged to accept a deal written into the law of public labor relations according to which they forfeited their right to strike in return for the right to bargain over the terms and conditions of employment. One of the most onerous of these laws, New York's Taylor Law, construes any concerted action that results in the withdrawal of labor, even if not sanctioned by the union, as a violation punishable by heavy fines and possible imprisonment if union leaders fail to order their members to cease and desist. Moreover, the law specifies allowable mandatory and nonmandatory subjects of bargaining. New York State and California have the highest concentration of unionized academics, accounting for about a quarter of the national total. Management must bargain with employees over salaries, benefits, and other terms and conditions of employment except those conditions not considered mandatory. Among the nonmandatory subjects is governance. Although all of the unions frequently invoke the traditional AAUP principle of "shared governance" (itself a compromise from the premodern concept that higher education was constituted as a community of scholars who shared administrative as well as instructional duties), the reality is that almost nowhere in the public sector does faculty have a legal or institutionally sanctioned right to negotiate over issues of governance, whether through unions or faculty senates. The senate has advisory status at best, but unions are barred from addressing the question of governance at the bargaining table. In the case of the prohibitions of the Taylor Law, the question of what constitutes "terms and conditions of employment" is becoming a hot topic.

Unions, even those not recognized by administrations for the purpose of collective bargaining, may be in the best position to take a stand because they can publicize the effects of administrators' unilateral actions (or actions taken in consultation with essentially powerless faculty senates dominated by administrators) and wage a campaign in the community, in the media, and among students to reverse them. Here are some examples of such actions:

- Devising protocols regarding intellectual property
- Closing down programs, as in the cases of library science and geography at Columbia in the 1990s
- Instituting online bachelor's degree programs, as at the City University of New York (CUNY)

- Raising "academic standards" for admission to a level that results in declining enrollments of black students and members of other ethnic-minority groups
- Instituting five-year tenure reviews for all faculty over the objections of faculty organizations, a "reform" that is already in effect on dozens of campuses in the private and public sectors
- Undertaking dismissal proceedings for dissenting professors or those suspected of cooperating with "terrorists" without proffering charges or observing other due process protections for the accused

Where unions do have bargaining rights, they should consider broadening their demands to include governance issues.

Beyond the inevitable resistance of administrations, boards of trustees, and legislatures to this admittedly novel redefinition of the role of academic unions, there are practical impediments. Coded as a "noneconomic" demand, the expansion of the right to bargain over issues that are reserved for administrations will encounter concern among members that economic issues might be sacrificed in the bargain. Moreover, even more than salary and benefit gains, the demand for power in the governance of the institution is likely to become a strike issue, especially if the other side takes the position that it will "never agree" to such an impudent demand. It would take a serious education campaign among faculty, union as well as nonunion, who either retain confidence in the faculty senate to address these issues or have been habituated to considering the union as they consider an insurance company: The bargaining committee and the leadership are responsible for "delivering the goods," principally salaries and health and pension benefits. And there will be problems with union leaders who share the members' predispositions or, if they grasp what is at stake in making these radical demands, lack confidence that the members will go to the barricades to win genuine participation in governance.

In public institutions the fight would of necessity have to be waged on several fronts, including a state legislature that is unlikely to receive the request for broadening faculty powers with sympathy. In order to achieve this goal, unions of professional staff, clerical workers, graduate students, and maintenance employees would have to be recruited to join in the fight. These unions and their members might actually believe that shared governance is none of their business. To convince them, faculty members would be required to alter their own attitudes and hierarchical values. Why should a registrar, program assistant, adjunct professor, or maintenance mechanic be interested in governance? One reply: In this era of relentless cost cutting and budget shortfalls, the entire community is affected by planned downsizing, by weakening faculty and staff power, and by the structural changes that occur more frequently. Another: If working in the university is not just a job but a career choice for most employees, being concerned with broader policy issues may be a vital matter not just for faculty but for all.

Prior to accepting an appointment at CUNY's Graduate Center, I worked at two major research universities: the University of California–Irvine (UCI) and Columbia. UCI has a very weak faculty union with no bargaining rights, but graduate assistants, clerical staff, and some administrative employees are unionized. Columbia underwent a fierce struggle to organize maintenance workers in the 1940s, and twenty years later clerical employees joined the ranks of organized labor. But, in the main, faculty members remain convinced that their interests are best served by relying on their individual merit. They sincerely believe that collective action may be appropriate for manual laborers and white-collar workers but that members of the academic elite are well advised to stay away from unions. But in the past twenty years, UCI, a public university, has been subject to several budget crises that have affected faculty members' salaries and, even more to the point, occasionally restricted access to research resources. The faculty senate seems powerless to address these issues effectively. At Columbia, a private institution, faculty has few levers to restrain administrative decisions to shut down, alter, or differentially support various programs or to impose its own tenure recommendations on an administration whose major goal is to restrict tenure to senior scholars recruited from outside. Like other Ivy League schools, Columbia regularly denies tenure to accomplished junior faculty on the theory that they should prove themselves elsewhere and come back as mature scholars.

I have no illusions that the most privileged members of the professoriate are prepared yet to recognize that they are really employees whose powers within the institution are limited. Yet if academic unions were to raise the ante on the terms and conditions of academic employment to include questions of governance, more than salaries and benefits, they might begin to persuade even the most individualistic of the faculty that there is a chance for faculty and staff empowerment. In any case, in public colleges and universities, pursuing this perspective is more than desirable: It is imperative.

◆

8

The Decline of Labor Education

I

These are hard times for worker and labor education. Universities almost everywhere are cutting back on staff and resources or, in some instances, eliminating once vibrant labor centers that provided indispensable instructional programs and research to workers and their unions. Union education departments, having long since confined their activities to training stewards and local union leaders in such day-to-day skills as grievance handling, local union administration, collective bargaining, and political action (how to mobilize members to support labor's legislative agenda and its endorsed—mostly Democratic—candidates), have either been pared to the bone or destroyed, sometimes on the argument that organizing should be the labor movement's sole or highest priority and that education is a luxury. In some cases, union leaders have claimed that in a time of severe budget crunch due in part to stagnant or declining membership and higher costs, the organization simply cannot afford education, however worthy the program may be.

Labor education is a tradition as old as the labor movement itself. At first its underlying premise was that the labor movement was the authentic site for workers' education. In the main, colleges and universities were places for the elite and the occasional talented student of working-class background. Moreover, many unionists distrusted a state that was capable of engaging in strikebreaking and politicians who talked from both sides of their mouths. Why should the political system be trusted to educate the working class, at least beyond the sixth grade? For these and other reasons, in the first half of the twentieth century, the socialist, communist, and militant industrial union movements conducted extensive education programs, both for their own members and for the communities in which they lived. In many industries the majority of workers were recent immigrants, so the unions offered classes in literacy as well as in labor history, strategy and tactics of the labor movement, and American law and political structure. Instructors taught English from labor and radical texts; the great classics of Western literature; textbooks from which students could learn the structure and function of government; and, of course, the newspapers, especially the flourishing leftist press. The combination of labor education and literacy fulfilled two aims: to help members and their families gain citizenship, and to build a cadre of rank-and-file leaders whose grasp of the larger economic, political, and cultural spheres would make them articulate leaders who could mobilize their shopmates to engage in strikes or demonstrations, conduct struggles on the shop floor, and also learn how to use their precious free time for self-development. My mother's Uncle George was a sewing-machine operator and union activist in the cloak and suit industry, but he was also an avid opera lover who owned two season tickets to the Metropolitan Opera, albeit in seats way up in the balcony next to God.

Before World War II, most union-negotiated agreements were at best documents that simply recognized the union as the representative of workers in matters of wages and working conditions. The contract might contain a statement prohibiting discrimination against union activists and define the scope of representation, but it covered little else. The education program had to be geared to issues of grievance resolution at the informal level, that is, shop-floor negotiations between the union steward and line supervisors and, when necessary, direct action by the workers themselves. The idea that grievances should be settled by lawyers or full-time union officials was as absurd as it was economically infeasible to the fledgling labor movement. Lawyers were employed to defend workers when they were arrested during strikes and demonstrations but were deemed hardly competent to run union affairs. Since most unions employed only a skeleton full-time staff, and most were assigned to organize the unorganized, the real burdens of everyday shop-floor labor relations fell on the shoulders of the rank and file. Workers had to learn the complexities of negotiating piece rates with line supervisors; how to resolve "beefs" about discharges and other disciplinary issues; and how to address health and safety issues such as overheated or underheated factories, badly functioning and dangerous machines, and speed-up and stretch-out pushes.

In fact, the best organizers are basically educators. In the ideal setting, their job is to provide a key core of worker activists with the tools in the law and the principles of union solidarity and knowledge that may enable them to persuade their shopmates that it is worth risking their jobs, or at least surrendering their hard-earned free time, to form a union. The organizer rarely performs the day-to-day tasks of organizing. She "trains" the in-shop committee to answer many of the relevant questions about what a union would look like after it gained recognition from the boss, and what it would be able to accomplish. And the committee itself becomes a collective educator: It is prepared, in the plant or office, to answer the inevitable employer antiunion propaganda that the union is an "outside" and disruptive force, that it takes your money but cannot deliver many benefits in return, or that its victory could force the company to move or go out of business. Sometimes the committee must address the charge that the union is strike-happy and that the workers may never recover their financial losses that result from long strikes.

The educational staff member in the era of socialist and social unionism was really a specific type of organizer who promoted the values of democratic, rank-and-file-run unionism among the already unionized as well as unorganized workers and, in the best-case scenario, provided language and other forms of intellectual knowledge to empower workers to take charge of their own unions. For example, many education programs ran classes in public speaking, how to run a union meeting, and how to write and edit a shop paper. Beyond trade unionism, in concert with the purposes of the socialist leadership, some labor education programs offered courses and distributed pamphlets on such topics as the political economy of capitalism, what socialism is, how labor can assume power over society, or how workers can address problems of social transformation. Before World War I, socialism was variously defined as a society in which political and economic power was in the hands of the producers of wealth, a "cooperative commonwealth" based broadly on the principle that the products of labor should be shared on a more or less equal basis, and democracy was crucially defined as a society in which workers—the overwhelming majority—made most of the important decisions affecting production and other aspects of social and political life and in which such amenities as education, health care, recreation, and culture are free to the individual, regardless of whether they are employed. The main division in the labor movement was between the socialist unions and the business unions, for which questions of social power were infinitely deferred because they accepted the prevailing economic status quo.

Needless to say, most unions were not socialist-minded or even social unions in the contemporary meaning of the term (concerned with social justice but not necessarily fundamental social transformation). The social union signifies that the problem of a fundamental social transformation has already been foreclosed by the hegemony of capitalist ideology. But the tacit acceptance of the status quo does not signal that there is little room for improvement in an admittedly flawed economic and political system. The more progressive unions still advocate for those at the bottom of the economic and occupational ladder. The mission of the social union is to seek justice at every level of the workers' lives: immigrant legalization; a living wage for all workers, not just union members; decent housing at affordable rents or mortgages; and quality schooling for workers' kids. On the other side, the building trade unions, for example, are usually in a protective mode and oppose further immigration even though, needless to say, most of their members were once immigrants themselves. They consistently argue that high wages will take care of social problems; thus, the business model—higher wages and benefits—is the heart of "modern" unionism. Unions such as the Teamsters, the East Coast Longshore, and many craft organizations have historically taken this position.

It may be argued that there were two major shifts from the social union model in the nature of labor and worker education. After the National Labor Relations Act (1935) legalized independent unionism (independent of company influence and control) and collective bargaining, by the end of World War II the contract and its enforcement had effectively displaced most wider concerns. By 1950 the typical union contract was filled with specific provisions concerning terms and conditions of employment and had the force of shop-floor law. As industrial unions organized perhaps a majority of workers in key manufacturing industries, with few exceptions union functions gradually narrowed to making sure that management observed the *contract*, and education departments generally confined their activity to training a cadre of front-line union leaders in the ins and outs of what became, in most cases, a complex legal document that required interpretation. Remarkably, many workers with little more than a grade school education became experts in this series of interpretive tasks. With nothing more than a union education program, they were transformed into veritable semioticians of the contract, their hermeneutic skills were finely honed, and in day-to-day grievance handling they exhibited wide-ranging rhetorical skills with which to represent their members. In the vernacular, they were inducted into the new profession of "shithouse lawyer."

The second change came during the 1980s. Borrowing loosely from the model proposed by A. J. Muste's 1920s and 1930s Brookwood Labor College, itself a variation of Oxford's Ruskin College in the United Kingdom, some unions, mainly in the newly organized public sector, turned from labor to "worker" education. But whereas Ruskin and Brookwood offered workers a humanistic stew of literature and social science in order to empower them culturally as well as to address political and economic concerns, the public sector unions turned to universities to offer degree programs for their members, mainly to assist them to upgrade their job status. The American Federation of Labor (AFL) model of the "business agent" or delegate spread to many public employees' and industrial unions. Union staffs had grown exponentially, and full-timers increasingly replaced rank-and-file shop- or office-floor leaders in the administration of the contract. Now lawyers invariably sat at the bargaining table and represented members at arbitration proceedings. Some even became union leaders. After the initial organizing upsurge, union members became *clients* of the full-time leadership, which adopted a service rather than a social union model of organization. The member became a recipient of union services and came to regard the union as an insurance company. "Worker education" was frequently farmed out to colleges and universities, which offered degree programs to public employees who needed credentials to win a degree of mobility. Some programs offered liberal arts associate or bachelor's degrees. In other cases, the universities offered labor studies programs through certificates rather than degrees. Rank-and-file unionists could take extension or continuing education courses in labor history, collective bargaining, and other related subjects and earn a certificate that might help them obtain full-time organizing or business agent jobs, either with unions or, in some cases, human resources departments.

As late as the 1970s, it was virtually mandatory for every international industrial union to support an educational staff. In large cities where union strength was substantial, such as New York, Chicago, Detroit, Philadelphia, or Saint Louis, many large locals employed education staff who, in addition to holding steward training classes taught by themselves or by labor program staffs of the universities, participated in political and organizing activities. To the extent that educators were extensions of the will of the union leaders, as the leaders settled into the service model, often against their will, education was seen as another "benefit" offered by the union. It had definite political uses because the 1980s began the long era of wage stagnation, and union leaders could point to their education programs as a benefit analogous to health care or pensions. As often as not, tuition for going to school was part of the contract and paid for by employers (in lieu of a portion of wages). Under these conditions, school substituted for the general rise in living standards, now effectively foreclosed by fiscal crises and alleged public antipathy to unions, especially in the public sector.

The demise and transfiguration of worker education are symptoms of the retreat of organized labor on almost every front. Some leaders have become obsessed with the numbers game. Their position is that union power rests on increasing the membership rolls; anything else is secondary. Moreover, many union leaders, although preaching militancy in organizing, do not give a "rat's ass" about union democracy and openly advocate a new social contract with employers that would entail a high degree of labor-management cooperation. Therefore, a politically and ideologically oriented education program is little more than a frill, or worse, might generate "unrealistic" expectations among the rank and file. These leaders have elevated the clientization of the membership to a union principle: Yes, provide legal, immigration, and grievance services to the members, and especially provide credential-driven opportunities for everything from general equivalency diplomas to master's degrees. Except for the occasional conference, any effort to empower the rank and file beyond the exigencies of the union contract is viewed with suspicion, even hostility.

II

The year 2007 marked the twenty-fifth anniversary of the City University of New York (CUNY) Centers for Worker Education, bachelor's and master's degree programs for working adults. The unique feature of the centers, which are located at New York's City, Brooklyn, and Queens Colleges, is that they were, and remain, underwritten, at least in terms of student enrollment, by some of New York City's public employees' unions. The combined enrollment for the three programs is more than 2,500, including some certificate and continuing education opportunities. Faculty is largely recruited from among the full-time staffs of the colleges, although Queens has employed a significant number of part-time instructors. In the main, the centers grant liberal arts degrees and, in some instances, professional degrees in areas such as early childhood education (so that assistant teachers in child care facilities may qualify as full-fledged teachers). At Brooklyn, the master's degree is in public administration, although the faculty interprets this specialization in broad social science terms. In one instance, Queens College, there are labor studies and urban studies options. But, with the exception of the Joseph Murphy Institute and Queens, which offer a labor studies certificate, the aim of the programs is not to focus on labor studies but to offer a broad curriculum in general higher education on the premise that public employees need credentials and exposure to literature, science, and social studies.

To celebrate this anniversary, the Brooklyn and City Centers for Worker Education held a conference on June 1 and 2, 2007, and invited labor educators from around the country to participate. Panels addressed many of the key issues in worker education, such as the current crisis in labor education. Numerous speakers reported retrenchment and even elimination of some of the more venerable and prestigious labor education centers, such as those of the University of California–Los Angeles; Indiana University; and Cornell University, which, according to one of its staffers, now charges individuals fees to attend seminars and labor breakfasts because of budget cuts that have resulted in layoffs and declining resources. Beyond questions of curriculum—what university and union worker education programs should offer to rank-and-file members—there was a well-attended session on "working-class consciousness" during which four speakers addressed the problem of workers' self-identification as "middle class" and concluded that, apart from the larger social reasons for this phenomenon, unions bear considerable responsibility for the decline of worker solidarity and political understanding. Other sessions asked what the new frontiers of worker education are. John Hyland, a retired LaGuardia Community College sociology professor and former treasurer of the Professional Staff Congress, the union of faculty and staff at CUNY, proposed a new approach that would focus on building neighborhood-based organizations. These groups might combine worker education and social action around local issues as well as participate in organizing. They would combine the efforts of several local unions whose members are concentrated in particular communities.

Despite its historical significance, the conference reflected the limits of present-day unionism. The reality is that unions are almost universally in a defensive mode; the idea that they can, even if they wished, overcome the old business union model seems unrealistic. In most instances, the best they can manage is to keep the flag of labor history, contemporary social and political education, and the fight for justice at the workplace flying, even if at half-mast. So the question arises: Is traditional schooling the only source of systematic education? If so, where are the forces for social transformation, if not the labor movement, broadly conceived? Can the social union model be revived, or is its demise in the postwar era in favor of what Robert Fitch has called the "clientization" of the membership (a model that is inferior to business unionism, which, at least in tendency, may entail militant struggle [Fitch 2006]) a sign that the once subversive function of labor education is deader than a doornail? The puzzle of the current era is that neither the service nor the business union models have been able to slow, let alone reverse, the decline of organized labor, both in membership and in social power. Recall when unions were strong—that is, when militant wage and benefits gains for members tended to lift the entire class. To stave off organization, employers tried to emulate some union standards because to refuse to do so might result in unionization of their workforce. Unions organized by pointing to this fact but argued that the gap between union and nonunion workplaces was still wide. Today, the gap between union and nonunion wages remains, although in this period of concessionary bargaining, it has narrowed considerably, robbing many organizers of their best argument. Workers still want to join unions, but in a time when unions cannot protect them from employers' wrath and cannot deliver on the economic front either, discretion is the better part of valor. Certainly, workers in and out of unions suffer long-term wage stagnation, an irreparable employer-based health care system, and a significant deterioration of workers' rights. Yet many union leaders refuse to change course except to engage in organizing, as if increasing the rolls will, by itself, lead to a reversal of fortune.

Even if, through some changes in the national administration and the law, labor regains some of its right to organize and bargain with employers, the experience of the last three decades since the beginning of the slide of union power suggests that, short of a revolt at the base of the labor movement—indeed, an effort to put the "movement" back into unions—inertia will prevail. The unions will continue on their current road. This prognostication is based on what I perceive to be the powerful force of habit among union administrations and the fact that many union leaders fear or for other reasons do not want a mobilized and educated membership. Even many socially minded union leaders cannot imagine a different regime of union administration. Some of the "progressive" unions are dead, meaning they go through the motions but lack imagination and a sense of dynamic possibility. For this reason, only a combination of internal and external pressure can create a change of course.

It is important to recall that the mass industrial union upsurge of the 1930s was not initiated by law. The labor relations law was, instead, a response to the mass strikes of 1933 and 1934, many led by labor radicals. Similarly, the second great wave, public employees' unionism of the late 1950s and 1960s, was spurred by the civil rights movement and later by feminism as well as by stirrings among a chronically underpaid workforce. In 2006, there were about sixty-five workers' centers around the country, almost none sponsored by conventional trade unions. The centers are not generally workplace based but instead are rooted in neighborhoods. They intervene about issues of housing, schooling, and problems of their members' workplaces. These organizations fight for labor and immigrant rights; assist workers who remain unpaid to gain their money through wildcat strikes; engage in legal interventions to thwart deportations and fight evictions; and conduct education programs among low-paid, mainly immigrant workers. In almost no cases do they seek or hold formal collective agreements with employers, single or otherwise. Is the future of the labor movement and of labor education this model of social centers? It is too early to tell, but the decline of the old contract unionism may give rise to new forms, of which the chronically underfunded workers' centers, which are based primarily where people live, are an alternative model.

As the AFL began to disintegrate under the weight of unprecedented political and industrial repression of the 1920s, many of its affiliates purged their ranks of communists and other radicals. In this environment, a new organization, the Trade Union Education League (TUEL), was born to ensure that radicals could continue to play a role in labor struggles. From 1923 through the early 1930s, TUEL remained an independent, effective force among workers in some industries, assisting strikes, demonstrations, and other activities. For a brief period, it transmogrified into a dual union that had some strength in textiles, mining, garments, electrical manufacturing, and the auto industry, among others, and played an important role in some struggles, particularly in textiles and mining. But with the rise of the Congress of Industrial Organizations and a change in Communist Party policy, it was folded into the new industrial union movement. I cannot rehearse the ideological problems of the organization, but recently some have suggested that a version of it might be appropriate for our times. Surely the labor movement needs a new burst of energy and imagination and a renewal of its historical mission to provide a counterhegemonic education for workers. How to initiate such a development is a vital component of labor's agenda.

PART III

TOWARD EDUCATIONAL RENEWAL

◇

9

Gramsci and Education

Published under the auspices of the Italian Communist Party after the war more than a decade after Antonio Gramsci's death in 1937, the celebrated *Quaderni* (prison notebooks) has not yet been fully translated into English. But the work has had an illustrious career since some pieces of it appeared in the late 1950s. The first of the translations were made by the Italian American trade union and political activist Carl Marzani and appeared under the title *The Open Marxism of Antonio Gramsci* in the wake of the Twentieth Congress of the Soviet Communist Party, at which, it will be recalled, Nikita Khrushchev revealed some of the crimes of Stalin. The significance of the convergence of Gramsci's first publication in English with that explosive speech can be grasped only when we understand the degree to which Gramsci's thought diverged from the orthodoxy Stalin had imposed on the world communist movement. Marzani's introduction of this hitherto obscure Italian Marxist thinker to English-speaking audiences was generally regarded as a "revisionist" document by both the orthodox Leninists and Gramsci's admirers. Gramsci's works seemed to vindicate the anti-Stalinist tenor of Khrushchev's main report to the congress and also, more to the point, suggested a departure from the prevailing Marxist-Leninist orthodoxy that had reigned for forty years.

Perhaps most salient was Gramsci's reconceptualization of civil society. Recall that in *Elements of the Philosophy of Right,* Hegel had made the radical argument that, rather than constituting a sphere of free discussion among equals, in the capitalist epoch every question resolved itself to the cash nexus. Consequently, civil society, which once promised a noncommodified environment for the development of a participatory (middle-class) citizenry, was coterminous with market relations. To the extent that Marx presupposed Hegel's distinction between state and civil society, now transmogrified into the binary categories of infrastructure and superstructure, the Marxist tradition tended to ignore the significance of the public sphere, including such institutions as media, voluntary organizations, and educational institutions. In contrast, Gramsci insisted that since all capitalist societies, even the fascist dictatorships, tend to rule primarily by consent rather than by force, the key to the rule of capital was to be found in its ability to achieve ideological hegemony over "civil society" conceived as the sphere of public life that was neither, strictly speaking, of the economy nor of the state. On the contrary, it was precisely the degree to which contending classes in modern society established their ability to create a "common sense" and thus appeared independent from the coercion of economic and state relations that their rule was made possible.

Marzani's slim volume of some of Gramsci's writings made little impact in the wake of the near collapse of the American and British Communist Parties in the late 1950s. But Gramsci's concepts of revolutionary politics were in sync with many in the New Left who, a few years later, sought an alternative Marxist tradition to that of Stalinism and even Trotskyism, which they viewed as authoritarian. Despite its fragmentary character, the most widely read of Gramsci's works is the second English-language selection, published in 1971 under the title *Selections from the Prison Notebooks.* Much longer and better annotated than the Marzani version, it stood alone until recently as a definitive scholarly rendition. Edited with a long introduction and copious notes by Quintin Hoare, it managed to provide most of Gramsci's central ideas by thematically dividing and synthesizing what were otherwise pithy notes, often provocative but sometimes banal. Despite Hoare's New Left credentials, the volume appeared under the imprint of the UK and U.S. Communist Parties' publishing houses and remains to this day the central source of the "popular" reception of Gramsci's thought. A companion volume extracted the large number of entries on culture. There now exist *Further Selections,* two volumes of the earlier political writings, the prison letters, and two volumes of a projected six-volume edition of the entire *Quaderni.* But the essays that mark Gramsci's most sustained contributions to philosophy; political, social, and cultural theory; and the strategy and tactics of revolutionary struggle are contained in the *Selections.*

Despite the diverse topics that occupied Gramsci's interest during his eleven-year internment (after all, he was himself trained as a "traditional," that is, humanistic intellectual, a designation that refuses the specialization that marks contemporary thought) and the obscurity of many of his references to contemporary Italian writers, most of whom have been long forgotten, activists as much as scholars still find much to fascinate them. Indeed, despite the virtual disappearance of official communism after the collapse of the Soviet Union in 1991, the commentaries continue on almost every aspect of his writings. What can the work of a general secretary of the Italian Communist Party whose major work was done during the fascist era say to us at a time when the political problematic to which Gramsci addressed himself seems to have been surpassed—a condition that perhaps was not evident in the immediate postwar years when the *Notebooks* were published? It is not only that the Soviet Union and its minions have disappeared from the world stage or that the Communist Parties of Eastern as much as Western Europe have degenerated into pale imitations of the social democratic formations they once despised. Or that what is left of official communism—Cuba, China, Vietnam, and North Korea—are social formations that, to say the least, have proven incapable of sustaining autarchic economies even as their political systems are, to one degree or another, Stalinist throwbacks, an asymmetry that is not likely to last. Equally to the point, a strong argument can be made for the historicity of many of Gramsci's formulations, especially his distinction between the war of position and the war of maneuver, where the latter signifies the strategy and tactics of revolutionary struggle. Although socialist revolution may not have been permanently foreclosed in Western countries, the prospects for such events seem dim, at least for the coming decades. What remains are the elaborations of the war of position—the long march through institutions in civil society and in struggles for intermediate power within the capitalist state, where my term "intermediate" signifies an extension of popular power from the institutions of civil society to the state, but still a capitalist state.

There is much in Gramsci's writings to mark him as a significant scholar. Let us stipulate at the outset that just as Marx was among the greatest Hegel commentators, Gramsci must be ranked as a major writer on Machiavelli. And his *Notes on Italian History,* especially his remarks on the so-called Southern Question, are a landmark in our collective understanding of why politics, even of

an international variety, must always take national and regional
specificities into account. Moreover, his contributions to the development of historical materialism, configured as a critique of
Nikolai Bukharin's attempt at a popular manual as well as his
other comments on the significance of culture and language in the
formation and reproduction of the nation-state (found chiefly in his
"Problems of Marxism"), are among the most powerful statements
of the nondogmatic Marxism that later transmuted into what
Perry Anderson called "western" Marxism (Anderson 1976). These
contributions richly deserve the scholarly attention the *Notebooks*
continue to receive even after the end of official communism.

There is, of course, a lively debate on Gramsci's ideas about
education. I would argue that his remarks on education and the
implicit educational issues addressed in many of his writings
remain among the most salient for us. In the United States, the
conversation has been conducted, in the main, among educational theorists and researchers who, given that they are largely
ensconced in universities and work at best within a reformist
environment, tend to focus on schools. Indeed, Gramsci's views
on the "common school" could easily be inserted into the contemporary curriculum debate. He insisted that the common school
should privilege "formative" rather than vocational and technical
education on grounds that are familiar today:

> The tendency today [in the public or common schools] is to abolish
> every type of schooling that is "disinterested" (not serving immediate
> interests) or "formative"—keeping at most only a small-scale ver-
> sion to serve a tiny elite of ladies and gentlemen who do not have to
> worry about assuring themselves of a future career. Instead there
> is a steady growth of specialized vocational schools, in which the
> pupil's destiny and future activity are determined in advance. A
> rational solution to the crisis ought to adopt the following lines.
> First, a common basic education, imparting a general, humanis-
> tic, formative culture; this would strike the right balance between
> development of the capacity for working manually (technically,
> industrially) and the development of capacities required for intel-
> lectual work. (Gramsci 1971, 27)

Gramsci's discussion is directed not only to the existing educational system but to what an educational system must provide
under conditions where the key institutions of the economy and
civil society are under popular control. Gramsci remarks that
contemporary "deliberative bodies" distinguish their work in two
"organic" spheres: The first is the essential decisions they must

make; the second is the "technical-cultural" activities under-taken by "experts" that precede decision-making. His reference to "deliberative bodies" signifies what popular or workers' coun-cils would have to consider in establishing common schools. Far from denigrating technical education, he calls for a balance so that those at the top levels of political leadership would possess familiarity with problems of production. Although the new soci-ety would inevitably require experts and he does not foresee the possibility of abolishing the capitalist division of labor anytime soon, Gramsci insists that "destiny" not be established at the out-set of a child's schooling by what we would now term "tracking" and that schools play a role in enabling manual and technical workers to engage in the intellectual work required of members of deliberative bodies that direct the system. In short, his posi-tion on the common school embodies his theory of democratic politics and his social philosophy, in which popular participation as well as representatives constitute the twin elements of any future democracy. His educational ideas are directed at improv-ing schools not so much for the sake of reform as for the sake of making possible a new kind of social rule in every institution of the state and civil society.

Gramsci devotes considerable attention to education, among other institutions, because even in the wake of fascism, schools are primary sites for achieving mass consent for social rule. The great Gramscian Louis Althusser argues that among the state's *ideological* apparatuses, as opposed to the *repressive* apparatuses (law, courts, police, army, prisons), educational institutions are the most important. The school is the state institution par excel-lence that prepares children and youth for their appropriate eco-nomic and political niches within the prevailing order (Althusser 1971). It acts as a sorting machine, forming and reproducing the classes of society according to what Pierre Bourdieu terms "de-grees of attainment of cultural capital." It transmits the dominant culture and habits of mind and, perhaps most important of all, inculcates in a large portion of the population the knowledges and values that are deemed appropriate for citizenship in a given social formation. But technical and manual workers are formed not only by specialized curricula (Bourdieu and Passeron 1977). A plethora of commentators, notably Paul Willis, have added that school "failure" is a crucial marker of working-class formation at the level of everyday life (Willis 1981). Manual or low-level ser-vice workers are formed by their refusal (coded as failure) of the standard curriculum that constitutes the basis for the accumulation of cultural capital.

Gramsci-inspired writers on schools in advanced capitalism have, with some notable exceptions, taken education to mean schooling. Although many writers have engaged in a sharp critique of the role and function of schooling in terms of what Henry Giroux and I have called "reproductive" theory, there is considerable reluctance to reveal the inner tensions of schools, that is, the degree to which movements within schools have attempted to offer both resistance and alternatives to the dominant program of technicization and the systematic devaluation of formative education (Aronowitz and Giroux 1985). Indeed, there is considerable evidence that many contemporary Gramscians recoil, on populist or libertarian grounds, at Gramsci's call for a curriculum that brings forward some of the features of the "old school of grammatical study of Latin and Greek together with the study of their respective literatures and political histories" (37). Gramsci extols the old school, admittedly reserved for a tiny elite, as a guide for a new common educational program:

> Individual facts were not learnt for immediate practical or professional end. The end seemed disinterested, because the real interest was the interior development of personality, the formation of character by means of the absorption and assimilation of the whole cultural past of modern European civilization. Pupils did not learn Latin and Greek in order to speak them, to become waiters, interpreters or commercial letter-writers. They learnt in order to know at first hand the civilization of Greece and of Rome, a civilization that was a necessary precondition of our modern civilization; in other words, they learnt them in order to be themselves and know themselves consciously. (37)

Gramsci defends the old common school for its ability to impart habits of "diligence, precision, poise (even physical poise), ability to concentrate on specific subjects, which cannot be acquired without the mechanical repetition of disciplined and methodical acts. If one wants to produce great scholars, one still has to start at this point and apply pressure throughout the educational system in order to succeed in creating those thousands or hundreds or even dozens of scholars of the highest quality which are necessary to every civilization" (37).

Clearly, if the criteria of contemporary relevance, of practical scientific and technical knowledge, and of specialization guide the educational system, these scholars are not likely to be produced, and the consequences for civilization would be deleterious. To form scholars, he argues, one must master more than one language and civilization in order to engage in the "analysis of distincts" (38), Croce's emendation of the dialectic to signify difference without contradiction. The student becomes an intellectual—no less than a scholar—by "plunging" into knowledge and life, by being subjected to the discipline of learning.

The old school was intended for the education of the ruling class. Its restriction to the upper reaches of society was intended not only to train succeeding generations of elites but to subject the subalterns to technical and vocational niches, a "destiny" that deprives them of the means by which any democracy may emerge. For Gramsci, democracy "by definition" means that the distinction between the ruler and ruled narrows, that "citizenship" beyond consent is broadened to mean active participation, is widely instituted. Yet, apart from providing in his prescription for school reform a common curriculum of early, disinterested education, he hesitates to draw the logical conclusion of his own analysis: the mass intellectual education of the subalterns. Or, in another locution of his terminology, the transformation of the masses from "spontaneous philosophers" to philosophically as well as technically educated social actors.

Gramsci despairs of translating old elite schooling to a mass education system, chiefly because workers and peasants lack the time and the cultural preconditions for study. Until the establishment of a new social order, his recommended strategy is to put education in the service of the formation of an intellectual "elite," where the concept of elite is transformed from its class-specific location in the traditional rulers to social groups in whose interest the formation of a new, egalitarian social order may come into being—the historical bloc of discontented social groups led by the working class. But short of an extensive program of formative schooling conducted by the revolutionary party itself, a task that may be necessary under conditions of the surrender of the public schools to occupational priorities, the struggle for reform of the common school curriculum in the direction of formative education is a necessary precondition for producing this elite.

Gramsci's concept of education is, however, only secondarily directed to schooling. The key is the formation of an "intellectual moral bloc" capable of contesting the prevailing common sense and providing in its stead, more or less systematically, a "scientific" understanding of the social world and of politics that can be widely disseminated in the institutions and other social spaces of civil society. Here the concept "science" signifies not the common usage of industrial societies, in which the object of knowledge is nature or a naturalized social world and the methods of knowing are experimental and mathematical, which strictly excludes intuition and speculation. Gramsci invokes a more traditional idea of science—the preindustrial, according to which science signifies only the effort to achieve systematic knowledge in which philosophy as much as the traditional natural and social sciences is a legitimate mode of knowledge acquisition.

Under the gaze of the censors, the term Gramsci employed to designate social science was "the philosophy of praxis." For nearly all commentators, it stood in for Marxism, and indeed, his texts provide some confirmation of this view. But there is a sense in which the philosophy of praxis may be understood as the unity of theory and practice. Unlike Leninist orthodoxy, in which theory is conceived as being in "the service" of practice, its "handmaid" or "guide," Gramsci understands the unity of the concepts as two sides of the same totality, and there is no structure of dominance. For, as his essays "The Study of Philosophy" and the compendium of comments from the *Notebooks* grouped under the title "Problems of Marxism" make clear, Gramsci's historical materialism and philosophy are directed principally and highly polemically against "mechanical materialism"—the dominant ideology of the Third, Stalinist International—especially ideas of historical inevitability with which Bukharin had, no doubt under pressure from Stalin, identified himself, as did many in the leadership of the Italian Communist Party. The philosophy of praxis is the core paradigm, if you will, from which the intellectual moral bloc needs to be formed to assist the masses to overcome the simple reductionism of bourgeois or Catholic common sense, both of which are content to leave them at a "low level" of understanding. The point of the bloc is "to make politically possible the progress of the mass and not only small intellectual groups":

> The active man-in-the-mass has a practical activity, but has no clear theoretical consciousness of his practical activity, which nonetheless involves understanding the world in so far as it transforms it. His theoretical consciousness can indeed be historically in opposition to his activity. One might almost say that he has two theoretical consciousnesses (or one contradictory consciousness): one which is implicit in his activity and which

in reality unites him with his fellow workers in the practical transformation of the real world; and one, superficially implicit or verbal, which he has inherited from the past and uncritically absorbed. It holds together a specific social group, it influences moral conduct and the direction of will ... but often powerfully enough to produce a situation in which the contradictory state of consciousness does not permit of any action, any decision or any choice, and produces a condition of moral and political passivity. Critical understanding of self takes place therefore through struggle of political "hegemonies" and of opposing directions, first in the ethical field and a higher level of one's own conception of reality. Consciousness of being part of a particular hegemonic force (that is to say political consciousness) in the first stage toward a further progressive self-consciousness in which theory and practice will finally be one. (333)

It is evident that the crucial educational issue is how to address the political hegemonies, how to bring the practical and theoretical consciousness of the most "advanced" political actors together. In short, beyond the "masses," how to overcome the power of common sense among those who are charged with political leadership within the great social movements. For Gramsci, the intellectuals are to be conceived not as the technicians of power but as its sinews. No class in modern society, he argues, can organize itself for power—for the war of maneuver, that is, the revolutionary activity—without the participation of intellectuals whose ultimate task is to embody the unity of theory and organization. It is they who contest in the institutions of civil society and the trade unions as well as the universities.

Which brings us to the central question of how to achieve scientific understanding in ever wider groups of the underlying population. In "The Modern Prince," Gramsci offers a particularly clear formulation of the task. He speaks of the need for "intellectual and moral reform" and suggests that the key is the development of a "national popular collective" that replaces the "divinity and the categorical imperative" by linking moral with economic reform. This at the cultural level.

But perhaps Gramsci's major innovation was to have recalled Machiavelli's insistence on the science of politics as an autonomous discourse and the idea that politics is the main science. Thus the struggle for a new scientific understanding as a new common sense always entails taking the point of view of "the man of action" rather than that of the scholar or, in current fashion, the nomadic intellectual.

◇

10

Paulo Freire's Radical Democratic Humanism

The Fetish of Method

The name of Paulo Freire has reached near iconic proportions in the United States, Latin America, and, indeed, in many parts of Europe. Like the cover comment by Jonathan Kozol on the U.S. edition of Freire's major statement *Pedagogy of the Oppressed* (1990), his work has been typically received as a "brilliant methodology of a highly charged political character." Freire's ideas have been assimilated to the prevailing obsession of North American education, following a tendency in all the human and social sciences, with methods—of verifying knowledge and, in schools, of teaching; that is, transmitting knowledge to otherwise unprepared students. Within the United States it is not uncommon for teachers and administrators to say that they are "using" the Freirean method in classrooms. What they mean by this is indeterminate. Sometimes it merely connotes that teachers try to be "interactive" with students; sometimes it signifies an attempt to structure classtime as, in part, a dialogue between the teacher and students; some even mean to "empower" students by permitting them to talk in class without being ritualistically corrected as to the accuracy of their information, their grammar, or their formal mode of presentation—or to be punished for dissenting knowledge. All of these are commendable practices, but they hardly require Freire as a cover.

Consequently, Freire is named a master teacher, a kind of Brazilian progressive educator with a unique way of helping students, especially those from impoverished families and communities.

The term he employs to summarize his approach to education, "pedagogy," is often interpreted as a "teaching" method rather than a philosophy or a social theory. Few who invoke his name make the distinction. To be sure, neither does the *Oxford English Dictionary*.[1] Yet a careful reading of Freire's work, combined with familiarity with the social and historical context within which it functions, obliges the distinction: Nothing can be further from Freire's intention than to conflate his use of the term pedagogy with the traditional notion of teaching. For he means to offer a system in which the locus of the learning process is shifted from the teacher to the student. And this shift overtly signifies an altered power relationship, not only in the classroom but in the broader social canvas as well.

This type of extrapolation is fairly typical of the U.S. reception of European philosophy and cultural criticism. For example, after more than a decade during which many in the humanities, especially literature, made a career out of working with the concept "deconstruction" as formulated by Jacques Derrida, treating the French philosopher as a methodologist of literary criticism, one or two books finally appeared that reminded the American audience that Derrida is, after all, a philosopher, and that his categories constituted an alternative to the collective systems of Western thought.[2] Some writers have even begun to grasp that Derrida may be considered as an ethicist. Similarly, another philosopher, Jürgen Habermas, has been taken up by sociology as well as by a small fraction of younger philosophers and literary theorists, and read in terms of their respective disciplines. What escapes many who have appropriated Habermas's categories is his project: to reconstruct historical materialism in a manner that takes into account the problem of communication, and especially the nonrevolutionary prospect of the contemporary world (Habermas 1979). Whether one agrees or disagrees with this judgment, the *political* configuration of his theoretical intervention ought to be inescapable, except for those bound by professional contexts.

None of these appropriations should be especially surprising. We are prone to metonymic readings, carving out our subjects to suit our own needs. In all of these cases, including that of Freire, there are elective affinities that make plausible the ways in which these philosophers and critics are read. For example, with the progressive education tradition, Freire rejects the "banking" approach to pedagogy, according to which teachers, working within the limits imposed by their academic discipline and training, open students' heads to the treasures of civilized knowledge. He insists that no genuine learning can occur unless students are actively involved, through *praxis,* in controlling their own education (here "praxis" is understood in the sense employed by several strains of Marxism—political practices informed by reflection). He is firmly on the side of a pedagogy that begins with helping students achieve a grasp of the concrete conditions of their daily lives, of the limits imposed by their situation on their ability to acquire what is sometimes called "literacy," of the meaning of the truism "knowledge is power." Freire emphasizes "reflection," in which the student assimilates knowledge in accordance with his or her own needs, rather than rote learning; he is dedicated, like some elements of the progressive tradition, to helping the learner become a subject of his or her own education rather than an object of the system's educational agenda. Like many progressives, Freire assails education that focuses on individual mobility chances while eschewing collective self-transformation.[3]

There are enough resemblances here to validate the reduction of Freire to the Latin John Dewey. Accordingly, if one adopts this analogy, his frequent allusions to revolutionary left-wing politics can be explained as a local phenomenon connected to the events of the 1960s and early 1970s, especially the advent in Brazil of the military dictatorship in 1964, the resistance to it, and the powerful popular social movements, particularly in Chile, with which he worked. Presumably, given a more thoroughly democratic context such as that which marks the political systems of North America and Western Europe, the core of Freire's teaching, the Method, would become apparent.

Similarly, while Dewey wrote on science, ethics, logic, and politics, among a host of other topics, outside the tiny band of Dewey specialists within schools of education, educational theory and practice routinely ignore the relationship between his general philosophical position and his education writings. And until very recently he was virtually unread by professional philosophers. Once at the center of American philosophy, his ideas have been deployed (in the military sense) by an insistent minority in full-scale revolt against the prevailing analytic school. Needless to say, just as Freire's revolutionary politics are all but dismissed in the countries where he has been elevated to a teacher-saint, Dewey's engaged political liberalism is generally viewed as a (surpassed) expression of the outmoded stance of public intellectuals at the turn of the century until the immediate postwar period. What can professional Dewey scholars say about his role in the founding of the American Federation of Teachers in 1916, or his role as chair of the commission that investigated the murder of Leon Trotsky?

Since American education has been thoroughly integrated into the middle-class cultural ideal that holds out the promise of individual mobility to those who acquiesce to the curriculum, engaged intellectuals like Dewey and Freire remain "relevant" to the extent that they can be portrayed within the dominant paradigms of the social sciences upon which educational theory rests. It is not surprising that Kozol can refer to Freire's "methodology," given the depoliticization of educational theory and practice in the United States; that is, the relative isolation of education issues, at least until recently, from the wider economic, political, and cultural scenes. Seen this way, his characterization of Freire as a "highly charged politically provocative character" seems almost an afterthought, or more to the point, a personal tribute not crucially intertwined with the "brilliant methodology."

Ivan Illich's statement on the same cover that Freire's "is a truly revolutionary pedagogy" comes closer to capturing what is at stake in his writing. The modifier "revolutionary" rather than "progressive" signifies an intention that is carefully elided by many of Freire's followers and admirers in schools. Or the term must be instrumentalized to mean that the pedagogy itself, as a methodological protocol, represents a radical departure from banking or rote methods of instruction. Therefore it is possible, if not legitimate, to interpret the significance of Freire's work not in the broader connotation of a pedagogy for life, but as a series of tools of effective teaching, techniques that the democratic and humanist teacher may employ to motivate students to imbibe the curriculum with enthusiasm instead of turning their backs on schooling.

True, Freire speaks of "method," especially in chapter 2 of *Pedagogy of the Oppressed*. In the early pages of this chapter, Freire seems to focus, in the narrow sense, on the "teacher-pupil" relationship as if to valorize the tendency of much educational theory toward microanalysis. For example, he provides a detailed "list" of characteristics of the banking method. Aside from obvious choices, such as who speaks and who listens, Freire makes his central point: "the teacher confuses the authority of knowledge with his own professional authority, which he sets in opposition to the freedom of the student." From this and the other specifications issues the conclusion that in the banking method "the teacher is the Subject of the learning process, while the pupils are the mere objects" (Freire 1990, 59).

To this "method" Freire counterposes "problem-posing education" where "men [sic] develop their power to perceive critically *the way they exist* in the world with which and in which they find themselves; they come to see the world not as a static reality but as a reality in the process of transformation" (Freire 1990, 71). This is where most American educators stop. Taken alone, the tacit thesis according to which Freire, notwithstanding his political provocation, is essentially a phenomenological progressive who uses language not too distant from that of psychologists working in this tradition, such as, say, Rollo May, seems to be justifiable. There is reference here to seeing life not as a static state of being but as a process of *becoming*. This spiritually laced education talk might be found as well in the writing of George Leonard and other American educators. American educators influenced by phenomenology are, typically, concerned with saving individuals from the dehumanizing effects of what they perceive to be an alienating culture. With few exceptions, they have adopted the implicit pessimism of most of their forebears which, despairing of fundamental social transformation, focuses on individual salvation.

But I want to argue that the task of this revolutionary pedagogy is not to foster critical self-consciousness in order to improve cognitive learning, the student's self-esteem, or even to assist in "his" aspiration to fulfill his human "potential." Rather, according to Freire,

> Problem posing education is revolutionary futurity. Hence it is prophetic.... Hence it corresponds to the historical nature of man. Hence it affirms men as beings who transcend themselves.... Hence it identifies with the movement which engages men as beings aware of their incompletion—an historical movement which has its point of departure, its subjects and its objective. (Freire 1990, 72)

It is to the liberation of the oppressed as historical subjects within the framework of revolutionary objectives that Freire's pedagogy is directed. The "method" is developed within a praxis, meaning here the link between knowledge and power through self-directed action. And contrary to the narrow, specialized, methodologically oriented practices of most American education, Freire's pedagogy is grounded in a fully developed philosophical anthropology, that is, a theory of human nature, one might say a secular liberation theology, containing its own categories that are irreducible to virtually any other philosophy. What follows is an account of this philosophical intervention and its educational implications.

Freire's Humanism

To speak of a philosophical anthropology in the era of the post-modern condition, and a poststructuralism which condemns any discourse that betrays even a hint of essentialism, seems anachronistic. Indeed, any superficial reading of Freire's work can easily dismiss its theoretical scaffolding as quaint, however much it may be sincere. For example, we read:

> The Pedagogy of the oppressed animated by authentic humanism (and not humanitarian) generosity presents itself as a pedagogy of man. Pedagogy which begins with the egoistic interests of the oppressors (an egoism cloaked in the false generosity of paternalism) and makes of the oppressed the objects of its humanitarianism, itself maintains and embodies oppression. It is an instrument of dehumanization. (Freire 1990, 39)

Now, we have already learned about the "fallacy of humanism" from the structuralists, especially Althusser and Lévi-Strauss. In Althusser's critique, humanism defines the object of knowledge, "man," as an essential being, subject to, but not constituted by, the multiplicity of relations of a given social formation (Althusser 1970). In adopting the language of humanism, Freire's debt to the early Marx and to Sartre is all too evident. He relies heavily on Marx, the Feuerbachian, whose materialism is severely tempered and reconfigured by a heavy dose of philosophical idealism. Recall Feuerbach's critique of religion, in which human suffering is displaced to God's will (Feuerbach 1957). Feuerbach argues that religion is made by humans and the problems to which it refers can only be addressed here, on earth. As if to underscore his own formation by this "flawed" tradition, Freire goes on to argue that the pedagogy he advocates addresses the problem of the authentication of humans by means of their self-transformation into a universal species:

> The truth is ... that the oppressed are not "marginals," are not men living "outside" society. They have always been "inside"—inside the structure that made them "beings for others." The solution is not to "integrate" them into the structure of oppression but to

transform the structure so they can become "beings for themselves." ... They may discover through existential experience that
their present way of life is irreconcilable with their vocation to
become fully human.... If men are searchers and their ontological
vocation is humanization, sooner or later they may perceive the
contradiction in which banking education seeks to maintain them
and then engage themselves in the struggle for their liberation.
(Freire 1990, 61–62)

Echoes of Hegelianism here. Freire invokes the familiar humanistic Marxian project: The revolution's aim is to transform what
Frantz Fanon terms "the wretched of the earth" from "beings for
others" to "beings for themselves," a transformation that entails
changing the conditions of material existence, such as relations of
ownership and control of labor, and the lordship-bondage relation
which is the psychosocial expression of the same thing.

Freire invokes the notion of the "ontological vocation" to become
human. In a brief dialogue with Lukács, who, in his tribute to
Lenin (Lukács 1970), endorses the role of the political vanguard
to "explain" the nature of the oppression to the masses, since
their consciousness has been victimized by commodity fetish-
ism, Freire emphasizes the idea of self-liberation, proposing a
pedagogy whose task is to unlock the intrinsic humanity of the
oppressed. Here the notion of ontological vocation is identical with
the universal, humanizing praxis of and by the most oppressed
rather than "for" them. For a genuine liberatory praxis does not
cease, even with the revolutionary act of self-liberation. The true
vocation of humanization is to liberate humanity, including the
oppressors and those, like teachers, who are frequently recruited
from among the elite classes to work with the oppressed, but who
unwittingly perpetuate domination through teaching.

Note here that Freire theorizes the class struggle, not as a
zero-sum game in which the victory of the oppressed constitutes a
defeat for the oppressor, but as a praxis with universal significance
and, more to the point, universal gain. For, as Freire argues, as
oppressors of their fellow humans, the "dominant elites" lose their
humanity, are no longer capable of representing the general will
to complete the project of humanization. *This* is the significance
of working with the most oppressed, who in Brazil and the rest
of Latin America are poor agricultural laborers and the unemployed huddled in the city's *favelas*, shantytowns, which in São
Paulo, for instance, harbor a million and a half people. Many of
these are migrants from forest and agricultural regions that are

in the process of being leveled for wood processing, mining and "modern" corporate farming.

As we can see in the citation above, Freire plays ambiguously with Marx's notion that the working class is in "radical chains." Where Marx sees the working class "in" but not "of" society, Freire insists they are "inside the structure" that oppresses them. As we shall see, this phrase signifies Freire's move toward psychoanalytic theory as a sufficient explanation of which material circumstances are the necessary conditions for accounting for the reproduction of class domination.

In the light of this admittedly humanistic discourse, what can be said about Freire's philosophy that rescues it from the dread charge of essentialism, and thereby relegates the entire underpinning of Freire's pedagogy to its own historicity? A closer examination of the crucial category of the "unfinished" shows the tension between his secular theology of liberation and the open futurity of the pedagogy. Taken at face value, "liberation," "emancipation," and "self-transcendence" are teleologically wrought categories that presuppose an outcome already present in the "project." In this aspect of the question, the goal, liberation, has the status of a *deus ex machina* of revolutionary action. For some critics, intellectuals, not the oppressed themselves, have designated the telos. It is intellectuals who have nominated themselves to deliver the subaltern from the yoke of material deprivation and spiritual domination. The oppressed must be the agent of universal humanization which, for Freire, is the real object of praxis. Taken at the surface of discourse, Freire can be indicted for reproducing the Leninist dictum according to which the task of the avant-garde intellectuals—in this case teachers—is to lead the masses into liberation.

But as we shall see, this judgment, however plausible, turns out to be misleading. I want to show that Freire's specific deployment of both psychoanalytic theory and phenomenological Marxism leads in exactly opposite directions. Moreover, Freire is aware that his rhetorical moves may easily be interpreted as another kind of elitism and takes up this issue. Freire's overt debt to Erich Fromm's psychological equivalent of material oppression, *the fear of freedom,* comes into play (Fromm 1940). Freire takes from Freud, Reich, and especially Fromm the insistence that oppression is not only externally imposed but that the oppressed introject, at the psychological level, domination. This introjection takes the form of the fear by members of the oppressed classes that learning and the praxis to which it is ineluctably linked will alter their life's situation. The implication is that the oppressed have an investment in their oppression because it represents the already-known, however grim are the conditions of everyday existence. In fact, Freire's pedagogy seems crucially directed to breaking the cycle of psychological oppression by engaging students in confronting their own lives, that is, to engage in a dialogue with their own fear as the representation within themselves of the power of the oppressor. Freire's pedagogy is directed, then, to the project of assisting the oppressed not only to overcome material oppression but also to attain freedom from the sado-masochism that these relationships embody. For Freire, profits and accumulation may account for exploitation of labor, but are insufficient explanations in the face of brutal domination. The dominating elites have a collective sadistic character corresponding to the masochism of the dominated. Freire quotes Fromm:

> The pleasure in complete domination over another person (or other animate creature) is the very essence of the sadistic drive. Another way of formulating the same thought is to say that the aim of sadism is to transform man into a thing, something animate into something inanimate since by complete and absolute control the living loses one essential quality of life—freedom. (Freire 1990, 45)

Freire goes on to say that "sadism is a perverted love—a love of death, not of life." The specific form of masochism is the "colonized man," a category developed by Frantz Fanon and Albert Memmi. Memmi (1973) argues that the colonized both hate and are fatally attracted to the colonizer. In the educational situation this takes the form of deference to the "professor"; the student may begin to generate themes but suddenly stop and say, "We ought to keep quiet and let you talk. You are the one who knows. We don't know anything" (Freire 1990, 50). Although Freire does not mention the term "masochism," that in this context manifests itself as the will to be dominated through introjecting the master's image of the oppressed, psychoanalysis insists that it is the dialectical inverse of sadism and that the two are inextricably linked. This introjection is, of course, the condition of consent, without which sadism could not exist without resorting to utter force to impose its will. Or, to be more precise, it would be met by resistance and a violence directed not horizontally among the oppressed, but vertically against the master.

It is not at all excessive to claim that the presuppositions of psychoanalytic theory are as fundamental to Freire's pedagogy as the existential Marxism that appears, on the surface, as the political and theological motivation of his discourse. For by positing the absolute necessity that the oppressed be self-emancipated rather than "led," on the basis of struggles around their immediate interests, by an avant-garde of revolutionary intellectuals, Freire has turned back upon his own teleological starting-point. For, the achievement of freedom, defined here as material, that is, economic and political as well as spiritual liberation, is a kind of *permanent* revolution in which the achievement of political power is merely a preliminary step.

Freire posits the absolute necessity of the oppressed to take charge of their own liberation, including the revolutionary process which, in the first place, is educational. In fact, despite occasional and approving references to Lenin, Freire enters a closely reasoned argument against vanguardism which typically takes the form of populism. In contrast to the ordinary meaning of this term in American political science and historiography, Freire shows that populism arises as a "style of political action" marked by mediation (he calls this "shuttling back and forth between the people and the dominant oligarchies" [Freire 1990, 147]). Moreover, he makes a similar criticism of some elements of the "Left" which, tempted by a "quick return to power," enter into a "dialogue with the dominant elites." Freire makes a sharp distinction between political strategies that "use" the movement to achieve political power (a charge often leveled against the Bolsheviks as well as the communist parties) and "fighting for an authentic popular organization" in which the people themselves are the autonomous sources of political decisions.

Freire's political philosophy, in the context of the historical debates within the revolutionary Left, is neither populist, Leninist, nor, indeed, social-democratic in the contemporary sense, but libertarian in the tradition of Rosa Luxemburg and the anarchists. Recall Luxemburg's sharp critique of Lenin's conception of the party as a vanguard organization, particularly his uncritical appropriation of Kautsky's claim that the working class, by its own efforts, could achieve merely trade union but not revolutionary consciousness. Inspired, in part, by Mao's conception of the *cultural* revolution, in which the masses are, ideologically and practically, the crucial force or the movement is nothing, Freire's pedagogy can be seen as a set of practices that attempts to specify, in greater concreteness than Mao did, the conditions for the fulfillment of this orientation.

Having proclaimed the aim of pedagogy to be the development of *revolutionary initiative from below,* Freire nonetheless rejects what he views as the two erroneous alternatives that have plagued the Left since the founding of the modern socialist movements: On the one hand, leaders "limit their action to stimulating . . . one demand," such as salary increases, or they "overrule this popular aspiration and substitute something more far reaching—but something which has not yet come to the forefront of the people's attention." Freire's solution to this antinomy of populism and vanguardism is to find a "synthesis" in which the demand for salaries is supported, but posed as a "problem" that on one level becomes an obstacle to the achievement of full "humanization" through workers' ownership of their own labor. Again, workers pose wage increases as a solution to their felt oppression because they have internalized the oppressor's image of themselves and have not (yet) posed self-determination over the conditions of their lives as an object of their political practice. They have not yet seen themselves *subjectively* (Marx 1975).

Freire's philosophy constitutes a tacit critique of poststructuralism's displacement of questions concerning class, gender, and race to "subject-positions" determined by discursive formations. The oppressed are situated within an economic and social structure, and tied to it not only by their labor but also by the conditions of their psychological being. The task of his pedagogy is to encourage the emergence of a specific kind of discourse which presupposes a project for the formation of subjectivities that is increasingly separate from that of the structure. Freire's construction does not *necessarily* repudiate the theoretical principle that the world and its divisions are constituted as a series of discursive formations into which subjects pour themselves. But he is addressing himself not to the bourgeois subject to which the old humanism refers—an individual "consciousness" seeking the truth through reason, including science—but to the possibility of working with a new problematic of the subject. Unlike twentieth-century Marxism, especially in Third World contexts, which accepts the ineluctability of domination based upon its position that underdevelopment breeds more or less permanent dependency (just as Lukács and the Frankfurt School essentially hold to reification as a permanent barrier to self-emancipation) in all of its aspects, Freire's is a philosophy of *hope.*

Recall Freire's statement, "problem posing education is revolutionary futurity." Its prophetic character crucially depends on specific interventions rather than declarations of faith. The teacher-intellectual becomes a vehicle for liberation only by advancing a pedagogy that decisively transfers control of the educational enterprise from *her- or himself* as subject to the subaltern student. The mediation between the dependent present and the independent future is *dialogic* education:

> Dialogue is the encounter between men [sic], mediated by the world, in order to name the world. Hence dialogue cannot occur between those who want to name the world and those who do not wish this naming—between those who deny other men [sic] the right to speak their word and those whose right to speak has been denied to them. Those who have been denied their primordial right to speak their word must first reclaim and prevent the continuation of this dehumanizing aggression. (Freire 1990, 76)

Thus, Freire's deployment of psychoanalysis is not directed toward *personal* liberation but instead to new forms of social praxis. The basis of this praxis is, clearly, the overriding notion that humans are an unfinished project. This project, for Freire, is grounded in his conception that to be fully human, in contrast to other species of animals, is to shed the image according to which only the "dominant elites," including leftist intellectuals, can be self-directed. His pedagogy, which posits the central category of *dialogue*, entails that recovering the voice of the oppressed is the fundamental condition for human emancipation.

From Revolution to Radical Democracy

I have deliberately abstracted Freire's social, psychological, and political philosophy from the social context in which it emerged in order to reveal its intellectual content. However, one cannot leave matters here. Without completely historicizing the significance of this intervention, we are compelled to interrogate this revolutionary pedagogy in the light of the sweeping transformations in world economic, political, and cultural relations, to re-place Freire's philosophy and pedagogy in the emerging contemporary world political situation.

Of course, I need not rehearse in detail here the extent of the changes that have overtaken revolutionary Marxism since, say, the fall of the Berlin Wall in December 1989. It is enough for our purposes to invoke the world-transforming events in Eastern Europe. They were simultaneously liberating—the Soviet Union and the nations of that region may be entering a new epoch of democratic renewal—and disturbing. We are witnessing the collapse of bureaucratic and authoritarian state rule in favor of liberal democracy, the emergence of capitalism, or at least radically mixed economies, but also nationalism, accompanied by a burgeoning anti-Semitism and racism, even signs of resurgent monarchism.

In Latin America, the site of Freire's crucial educational practice, not only in his native Brazil but also in pre-Pinochet Chile, revolutionary perspectives have, to say the least, suffered a palpable decline, not only after the defeat of the Sandinistas in the Nicaraguan election, but also in the choice by much of the erstwhile revolutionary Marxist Left to place the struggle for democracy ahead of the class struggle and the struggle for socialism. Some have even theorized that, despite deepening poverty and despair for much of the population, socialism is no longer on the immediate agenda of Latin American societies in the wake of the world shifts that have decimated their economies, shifts that also encourage the formation of totalitarian military dictatorships. In this environment, recent political liberalizations have shown themselves to be fragile. For example, presidential democratic regimes in Argentina and Chile had hardly taken root before the military threatened to resume power to restore "law and order."

Some political theorists of the Left, notably Norberto Bobbio, have forcefully and influentially argued that parliamentary democracy within the framework of a mixed economy dedicated to social justice is the farthest horizon of socialist objectives (Bobbio 1987a and 1987b). Following him, many leaders of the Brazilian Left have acknowledged the limits of political transformation under conditions of underdevelopment. Others, while agreeing with the judgment according to which the revolutionary insurgencies of the 1960s and 1970s were profoundly misdirected, dispute Bobbio's thesis that *radical* democratic perspectives suffer from romantic nostalgia and would inevitably fail. What is important here is, in either case, a decisive skepticism concerning the prospects for revolutionary socialism, at least for the present.

Which raises the question of whether there can be a revolutionary pedagogy in nonrevolutionary societies. Is it not the case that Freire's philosophy has been historically surpassed even if, in the context of its formation, it possessed the virtues of perspicacity? Under present circumstances, is it not enough to preserve Freire's work in a more modest form, as a teaching method? To be sure, Freire himself is excruciatingly aware of the changed circumstances of the late 1980s and the 1990s. On the occasion of his appointment to the post of secretary of education for the newly elected Workers' Party (PT) municipal administration in São Paulo, Freire told an interviewer that he saw in this unexpected victory "a fantastic possibility for at least changing a little bit of our reality" (Williams 1990). The prospect for this radical left democratic administration was to achieve some reforms in health, transportation, and education. His perspective in accepting the post was to "start the process of change" during the PT's four years of elective office.

Even before assuming office, Freire was aware of the severe limits to change posed by the economic and political situation. But he was also facing schools in which 60 to 70 percent of students dropped out and had barely four years of schooling, the majority of whom will be day laborers working for minimum wages. He was responsible for thirty thousand teachers in the city's school system, many of whom lacked training for the awesome task of helping students break from the fatalism of Brazilian society.

In 1990, after a year of reform, Freire and his associates were speaking about democracy—social democracy—rather than "revolution" in the strict political sense. The term "popular democratic school" is counterposed to the "capitalist" school. The capitalist school "measures quality by the quantity of information it transmits to people," says Freire's associate, Gadotti (Williams 1990). The popular school, on the other hand, measures quality by "the class solidarity it succeeds in establishing in the school." In order to achieve this objective the school must be "deformalized," debureaucratized, a measure that entails democratizing schools so that "the community" elects the school director, and there is direct accountability. This means the director can be removed at any time by the base, but also that curriculum and other decisions are broadly shared. Freire uses the term "accountability" to describe this desired relationship.

In the postdictatorship period, one might say in the postcolonial situation, the popular-democratic philosophy has not changed, but the discourse is now eminently practical: As a schools administrator Freire speaks the language of praxis, rather than merely invoking it. The PT and its education secretary must address issues of teacher training, school-based decision-making, administration and curriculum, but from the base of a *working-class-oriented political formation that holds radical democratic reform toward popular power as its core ideology.* Freire is still trying to transfer power to the oppressed through education, now framed in the context of state-financed and -controlled schooling.

Sharing Power

In his "spoken" book with Antonio Faundez, *Learning to Question* (1989), prepared before the PT victory, Freire had already altered his discursive practice. Throughout the text, Freire returns to the vexing relation between theory, ideological commitment, and political practice. Here I want to give just one example of the degree to which his fundamental framework remains constant, even in the wake of the shift from revolutionary to democratic discourse. In one section Faundez and Freire engage in fascinating dialogue on intellectuals.

Faundez begins by reiterating a fairly well-known Marxist idea: that there is a social "science," a body of knowledge which is not merely descriptive of the present state of affairs, but "guides all action for social change, how can we ensure that this scientific knowledge ... actually coincides with the knowledge of the people" (Freire and Faundez 1989, 55–56). At this point Faundez contrasts the science possessed by intellectuals with the "ideology" of the dominant classes that suffuses the people's knowledge, as well as the diverse elements of practical knowledge, inconsistency between theory and practice, and so forth. The intellectuals as bearers of science find themselves caught in an excruciating paradox. On the one hand, they are bearers of scientific knowledge, owing not so much to their talent as to their social position which gives them access to it. On the other hand, only by merging their science with the internalized knowledge of the people and, more particularly, fusing their vision of the future with popular imagined futures can the elitism of the various political vanguards be avoided.

As in most leftist discussions of intellectuals, Faundez draws from Gramsci's undeniably pioneering writings, especially themes which Mao and Foucault are later to elaborate and develop: that all knowledge is specific, and that it is situated in a national context.

Freire responds by objecting to the view that the future is *only* particular. He wants to preserve the universal in the particular, and argues that we already have, in outline, a vision. But the nub of the problem remains: Are the radical intellectuals prepared to share in the "origination" of new visions with the masses, or are these fixed so that the problem of coincidence is confined to strategy and tactics? Freire presses Faundez here to clarify the role of intellectuals in relation to the popular movements. Freire is plainly uneasy with the formulation that intellectuals are the chief bearers of scientific knowledge, and wants to assert that, to achieve radical democratic futures, a fundamental shift in the relationship between intellectuals, especially their monopoly over scientific knowledge, and the movements must take place. Moreover, he is concerned to remove the curse, "bourgeois," from the concepts of democracy. A radical democracy would recognize that there are no fixed visions. And if visions are fashioned from knowledge of the concrete situations gained through practice, there can be no science that provides certitude, in its categories, its descriptions, much less its previsions.

Reporting on a conversation with workers' leaders in São Paulo, Freire *defines* class consciousness as the power and the will by workers and other oppressed and exploited strata to *share* in the formulation of the conditions of knowledge and futurity. This demand inevitably alters the situation of power: Intellectuals must be consistent in the translation of their democratic visions to practice. In other words, they must share the power over knowledge, share the power to shape the future.

This exchange is a meditation on Latin American revolutionary history and current political reality, most especially the failure of Leninist versions of revolutionary Marxism and socialism. Explicitly, Freire warns against defining the goal of radical movements exclusively in terms of social justice and a more equitable society, since these objectives can conceivably be partially achieved without shared decision-making, especially over knowledge and political futures. *The key move away from the old elitist conception in which the intellectuals play a dominant role is to challenge the identity of power with the state.* Faundez sets the stage for this shift:

> I think that the power and the struggle for power have to be rediscovered on the basis of resistance which makes up the power of the people, the semiological, linguistic, emotional, political and cultural expressions which the people use to resist the power of

domination. And it is beginning from the power which I would call primary power, that power and the struggle for power have to be rediscovered. (Freire and Faundez 1989, 64)

Freire's reply sets a new ground for that rediscovery. Having focused traditionally on workers' and peasant movements, he now enters significantly into the debates about the relationship between class and social movements. He names movements of the urban and rural poor who, with the assistance of priests from the liberationist wing of the Catholic Church, began in the 1970s to redefine power as the power of resistance. But he goes on to speak of movements of "environmentalists, organized women and homosexuals," as "new" social movements whose effectivity must inexorably influence the strategies of the revolutionary parties:

> It is my opinion today that either the revolutionary parties will work more closely with these movements and so prove their authenticity within them—and to do that they must rethink their own understanding of their party, which is tied up with their traditional practice—or they will be lost. Being lost would mean becoming more and more rigid and increasingly behaving in an elitist and authoritarian way vis à vis the masses, of whom they claim to be the salvation. (Freire and Faundez 1989, 66)

With these remarks, Freire distances himself from elements of his own revolutionary Marxist past, but not from a kind of open Marxism represented by Gramsci's work. For there can be no doubt that this comment is directed towards those in the revolutionary Left for whom class defines the boundaries of political discourse. Without in any way renouncing class as a fundamental category of political struggle, Freire places himself in the company of those theorists, some of whom are situated in the social movements and not within the parties, who have challenged the priority of class over other social categories of oppression, resistance, and liberation. His intervention is also postmodern when he puts into question the claim of political parties to "speak in behalf of a particular section of society." In his latest work Freire takes a global view, integrating the democratic ideology of the Guinea-Bissauan leader Amilcar Cabral, with whom he had forged a close relationship.

Freire is sympathetic to Faundez's reminder that knowledge and its bearers are always specific, that historical agency is always situated in a national context. Yet, with Cabral, he reiterates the need to "overcome" some features of culture. This overcoming means that tendencies towards the valorization of "localism," which frequently are merely masks for anti-intellectualism among populist-minded leaders, should be rejected. So Freire's postcolonial, postmodern discourse does not sink into the rigidities that have frequently afflicted these perspectives. Finally, at the end of the day, we can see that to appreciate difference does not resolve the knotty issues of judgment. Freire is an implacable opponent of bureaucracy that throttles popular initiative, but suggests that workers for social change must retain their "overall vision" (Freire and Faundez 1989, p. 123).

Redefining power democratically entails, at its core, interrogating the concept of "representation." The claim of revolutionary parties to represent workers, the masses, the popular majority, rests in the final analysis on the status, not of the demand for social justice, for liberal parties may, under specific conditions, also make such claims. Instead, it rests on the rock of scientific certainty, at least as to the descriptive and prescriptive propositions of a body of knowledge whose bearers, the intellectuals, thereby legitimate their own right to leadership. Freire's call for *sharing* recognizes the unique position of intellectuals in the social and technical division of labor, and thereby disclaims the stance of populism that almost always renounces the role of intellectuals in social movements, and with that renunciation is left with a vision of the future in the images of the present. But, by breaking with the "state," that is, coercion and representation as its key features, it also rejects the notion that liberation means the hegemony of intellectuals—political, scientific, cultural—over the movements.

In this way, any attempt to interpret Freire's recent positions as a *retreat* from the revolutionary pedagogy of his earlier work is entirely unjustified. On the contrary, Freire reveals his undogmatic, open thought in his most recent work. In fact, it may be argued that the Christian liberation theology of the past two decades is a kind of vindication of his own secular theology, with its categories of authenticity, humanization, and self-emancipation. The paradoxes in his political thought are not apparent, they are real. For like the rest of us, Freire is obliged to work within his own historicity, an "overall vision" that is at once in global crisis, and remains the only emancipatory vision of a democratic, libertarian future we have.

Notes

1. "Pedagogy—the work or occupation of teaching … the science or art of teaching." *Oxford English Dictionary* (complete edition) (New York: Oxford University Press, 1971), p. 604.

2. See, especially, Stephen W. Melville, *Philosophy Beside Itself: On Deconstruction and Modernism* (Minneapolis: University of Minnesota Press, 1986).

3. John Dewey himself is a model for the idea of *collective* self-transformation; see his *Democracy in Education* (Glencoe, Illinois: Free Press, 1959).

References

Althusser, Louis. 1970. *For Marx.* New York: Vintage.
———. 1971. "Ideology and Ideological Apparatuses." In *Lenin and Philosophy.* New York: Monthly Review Press.
Anderson, Perry. 1976. *Considerations on Western Marxism.* London: New Left Books.
Arendt, Hannah. 1958. *The Human Condition.* Chicago: University of Chicago Press.
———. 1961. "The Crisis in Education." In *Between Past and Future.* New York: Penguin Books.
Aronowitz, Stanley. 1973. *False Promises: The Shaping of American Working Class Consciousness.* New York: McGraw-Hill.
———. 1984. "When the New Left Was New." In *The 60s Without Apology,* ed. by Sonhya Sayres, Anders Stephanson, Stanley Aronowitz, and Fredric Jameson. Minneapolis: University of Minnesota Press.
———. 1996. *Death and Rebirth of American Radicalism.* New York: Routledge.
———. 2000. *The Knowledge Factory: Dismantling the Corporate University and Creating True Higher Education.* Boston: Beacon Press.
Aronowitz, Stanley, and William DiFazio. 1994. *The Jobless Future.* Minneapolis: University of Minnesota Press.
Aronowitz, Stanley, and Henry Giroux. 1985. *Education Under Siege.* South Hadley, MA: Bergin and Garvey.
Bazin, André. 1989 [1961]. *What Is Cinema?* Berkeley: University of California Press.
Berube, Michael, and Cary Nelson. 1994. *Higher Education Under Fire.* New York: Routledge.
Blum, Linda. 1991. *Between Feminism and Labor: The Significance of Comparable Worth.* Berkeley: University of California Press.
Bobbio, N. 1987a. *Future of Democracy.* Minneapolis: University of Minnesota Press.
———. 1987b. *Which Socialism?* Minneapolis: University of Minnesota Press.
Bourdieu, Pierre, and Jean-Claude Passeron. 1977. *Reproduction in Education, Culture and Society.* London: Sage Publications.

Brint, Steven, and Jerome Karabel. 1989. *The Diverted Dream: Community Colleges and the Promise of Educational Opportunity in America.* New York: Oxford University Press,.

Christgau, Robert. 2001. *Any Old Way You Choose It.* Cambridge, MA: Harvard University Press.

Cicourel, Aaron, and John Kitrae. 1963. *The Education Decision-Makers.* New York: Bobbs-Merrill.

Dewey, John. 1980 [1916]. *Democracy and Education.* Carbondale: Southern Illinois University Press.

Du Bois, William Edward Burkhardt. 1903. *The Souls of Black Folk.* Chicago: A. C. McClung.

Elman, Richard M. 1966. *The Poorhouse State: The American Way of Life on Public Assistance.* New York: Pantheon Books.

Feuer, Lewis. 1969. *The Conflict of Generations: The Character and Significance of Student Movements.* New York: Basic Books.

Feuerbach, L. 1957. *The Essence of Christianity.* New York: Harper Torchbooks.

Fink, Leon, and Brian Greenberg. 1989. *Upheaval in the Quiet Zone: A History of Local 1199.* Urbana: University of Illinois Press.

Fisher, Donald. 1993. *Fundamental Development of the Social Sciences: Rockefeller Philanthropy and the United States Social Science Research Council.* Ann Arbor: University of Michigan Press.

Fitch, Robert. 2006. *Solidarity for Sale: How Corruption Destroyed the Labor Movement and Undermined America's Promise.* New York: Public Affairs.

Freire, P. 1990. *Pedagogy of the Oppressed.* New York: Continuum.

Freire, P., and A. Faundez. 1989. *Learning to Question: A Pedagogy of Liberation.* New York: Continuum.

Friedman, Thomas. 2005. *The World Is Flat: A Brief History of the Twenty-first Century.* New York: Farrar, Straus, and Giroux.

Fromm, E. 1940. *Escape from Freedom.* New York: Holt, Rinehart and Winston.

Fukuyama, Francis. 1992. *The End of History and the Last Man.* New York: Free Press.

Giroux, Henry. 2000. *Stealing Innocence: Youth, Corporate Power, and the Politics of Culture.* New York: St. Martin's Press.

Gompers, Samuel. 1924. *Seventy Years of Life and Labor: An Autobiography.* New York: E. P. Dutton.

Goodman, Paul. 1959. *Growing Up Absurd.* New York: Random House.

Gramsci, Antonio. 1971. *Selections from the Prison Notebooks,* ed. and trans. with an introduction by Quintin Hoare. New York: International Publishers.

Habermas, J. 1979. "The Reconstruction of Historical Materialism." In *Communication and the Evolution of Society.* Boston: Beacon Press.

Hardt, Michael, and Antonio Negri. 1994 [1890]. *Labor of Dionysus.* Minneapolis: University of Minnesota Press.

Heidegger, Martin. 1968. *What Is Called Thinking?* New York: Harper and Row.

Horkeimer, Max, and Theodor Adorno. 2002. *Dialectic of the Enlightenment,* trans. by Edmund Jephcott. Palo Alto, CA: Stanford University Press.

James, William. 1890. *Principles of Psychology.* New York: H. Holt.

Kael, Pauline. 1994. *I Lost It at the Movies.* New York: Marion Boyers.

Katz, Michael B. 1970. *The Irony of Early School Reform: Educational Innovation in Mid-Nineteenth-Century Massachusetts.* Boston: Beacon Press.

Kenney, Martin. 1986. *The University/Industrial Complex.* New Haven: Yale University Press.

Kerr, Clark. 1972. *The Use of the University.* New York: Harper and Row.

Kracauer, Siegfried. 1995. *The Mass Ornament.* Cambridge, MA: Harvard University Press.

Krause, Paul. 1992. *The Battle for Homestead.* Pittsburgh: University of Pittsburgh Press.

Lichtenstein, Nelson. 1996. *The Most Dangerous Man in Detroit: Walter Reuther and the Fate of American Labor.* New York: Basic Books.

Locke, John. 1954. *An Essay Concerning the Human Understanding.* New York: Dover.

Lucas, Christopher J. 1994. *American Higher Education: A History.* New York: St. Martin's Press.

Lukács, G. 1970. *Lenin.* London: New Left Books.

Lynd, Robert S. 1964 [1939]. *Knowledge for What? The Place of Social Science in American Culture.* New York: Evergreen.

Macdonald, Dwight. 1983. *Against the American Grain.* New York: Da Capo Press.

Marcus, Greil. 1975. *Mystery Train.* New York: Random House.

Marcuse, Herbert. 1964. *One-Dimensional Man.* Boston: Beacon Press.

Marx, K. 1975. "Thesis on Feuerbach." In *Early Writings,* ed. D. Fernbach. New York: Vintage.

McLaren, Peter. 1999. *Schooling as a Ritual Performance.* Lanham, MD: Rowman and Littlefield.

McLuhan, Marshall. 1964. *Understanding Media.* New York: McGraw-Hill.

Memmi, A. 1973. *The Colonizer and the Colonized.* New York: Holt, Rinehart and Winston.

Metz, Christian. 1991. *Film Language: A Semiotics of the Cinema.* Chicago: University of Chicago Press.

Mills, C. Wright. 1956. *The Power Elite.* New York: Oxford University Press.

Postman, Neil. 1986. *Amusing Ourselves to Death.* New York: Viking.

Powdermaker, Hortense. 1950. *Hollywood: The Dream Factory.* Boston: Little, Brown.

Ross, Andrew. 2003. *No-Collar: The Humane Workplace and Its Hidden Costs.* Philadelphia: Temple University Press.

Sennett, Richard, and Jonathan Cobb. 1973. *The Hidden Injuries of Class.* New York: Vintage.

Slaughter, Sheila, and Larry Leslie. 1997. *Academic Capitalism: Politics, Policies, and the Entrepreneurial University.* Baltimore, MD: The Johns Hopkins University Press.

Spivak, Gayatri. 1988. "Can the Subaltern Speak?" In *Marxism and the Interpretation of Culture,* ed. by Cary Nelson and Larry Grossberg. Urbana: University of Illinois Press.

Teitelbaum, Kenneth. 1995. *Schooling for "Good Rebels": Socialism, American Education, and the Search for Radical Curriculum.* New York: Teachers College Press.

Trachtenberg, Alan. 1988. *The Incorporation of America.* New York: Hill and Wang.

Veblen, Thorstein. 1993 [1918]. *The Higher Learning in America.* New Brunswick, NJ: Transaction Books.

Walsh, Sharon. 1994. "Berkeley Denies Tenure to Scientist Who Criticized Ties to Industry." *Chronicle of Higher Education* 50, 18 (January).

Williams, E. 1990. Interview with Paulo Freire, São Paulo.

Willis, Paul. 1981. *Learning to Labor: How Working Class Kids Get Working Class Jobs.* New York: Columbia University Press.

Index

186 *Index*

Morrell Act (1862), 66, 81
Multiversity, 63, 110, 116
Mulvey, Laura, 34
Music, 31, 32–33, 34
Muste, A. J.: model by, 143

Nasaw, David, 9
National Education Association
  (NEA), 105, 121
National Institutes of Health, 70;
  contracts by, 107; dedicated
  research and, 85
National Labor Relations Act
  (1935), 142
National Labor Relations Board,
  xvii
National Science Foundation:
  contracts by, 107; dedicated
  research and, 85; funds from,
  84
National security, 82, 85, 86
Natural sciences, 158; salaries
  in, 94
Nelson, Cary, xvii
Neoliberalism, xvii, xviii, 52, 56,
  62, 67, 76
New Deal, 8, 90, 108, 114
New economy, 29, 30
New Left, 99; free universities
  and, 39–40; revolutionary
  politics and, 152; university
  reform and, 110
New York City Board of
  Education, 6, 49
New York City Department of
  Education, 17–18, 49
New York Times, 116; news media
  and, 35; on rejection rates, 69
No Child Left Behind, xiii, xviii, 8
Notebooks (Gramsci), 153, 154, 158
Novartis, UC-Berkeley and, 86

Occupational outcomes, 54, 71
Old school, 156, 157
Opportunity, 18, 78; equality of,
  19, 21, 63; performance and, 27

Oppression, 168, 169, 170
Organization, xix, 114, 142; right
  to, 147; social, 16; social union
  model of, 143; structural, xii
Outsourcing, xv, 79, 81, 91

Palme, Goran: acts of solidarity
  and, 96
Parent-teacher associations, 78
Park East High School, 8; staff
  at, 6–7
Parsons, Talcott, 5
Pedagogy, xiii, 21, 94, 163, 164,
  165, 166, 167, 169; aim of,
  170–171; authoritarian, 64;
  changing, 50; child-centered,
  17; curriculum and, 118;
  faculty and, 118; futurity of,
  168; hidden, 28; improving,
  126; revolutionary, 172, 173,
  178; as social theory, 162;
  teaching and, 162
Pedagogy of the Oppressed
  (Freire), 161, 164
Peer pressure, 43, 44, 47–48
Performance, 17, 28, 29; black
  students and, 43–44; genetics
  and, 22; opportunity and, 27;
  working-class students and, 10
Pharmaceutical corporations,
  partnerships with, 82
Political control, 75
Political education, 31, 146
Political liberalism, 163, 173
Political power, 38, 170
Politics, higher education and, 62
Popular culture, 19, 50;
  commodification of, 34–35;
  counterknowledge of, 33; media
  and, 31–38; school and, 32
Popular movements, 176
Popular school, 174
Populism, 30, 171, 178
Poststructuralism, 166, 171
Poverty, xi, xiii, 27, 51
Powdermaker, Hortense, 34